"Somehow Dave has always been able to take even the most complicated song idea and turn it into a clear and moving message. In this book he has done just that—no wasted words, no useless information. Instead, it is right to the point, right to the heart. A true road map for worship pastors, with great directions for every turn along the way."

—MARK HARRIS
4HIM

"My friend, Dave Clark, writes, 'When I first began working on this book, I wrote down three goals—three words—on a piece of paper that I hoped to accomplish in these pages. The first of these words is *educate.*' That is precisely what Dave does in *Worship Where You're Planted.* Through his studies at Nazarene Bible College, Dave has demonstrated his commitment to preparation through education. This book will be a timely and valuable resource for those who plan and lead worship in the local church. Dave writes from a life of experience and expertise in leading people into the 'golden hour' of worship."

—HAROLD B. GRAVES JR.
President, Nazarene Bible College

"[Dave Clark's] perception is enlightened. His heart for the church is clearly evident. As I read this book, I repeatedly smiled as I thought 'If *only* this had been around when I started out!' Insightful and anointed, this is a *must* for any worship leader!"

—RUSSELL MAULDIN
Composer, Arranger

"Where was this book forty years ago when I was first called into the music ministry? It's such a great tool for the full-time, the part-time, the trained, or the untrained minister of music. With God and His Word as your guide, keep this book handy for those many questions that will arise in your ministry."

—DIANE M. HALL
Choral Music Consultant, Christian Supply

"In *Worship Where You're Planted,* Dave aims to educate, engage, and encourage those who lead God's people in praise and thanksgiving. He does not merely reach his goals, he exceeds them. When you read this book, you too will become inspired by stories from Dave's years of music ministry. But prepare yourself; you might also feel challenged by his insights. Dave Clark reminds us that genuine worship is not an event and it's not about us. Authentic worship is about our response to a gracious God. Dave stirs us to seize every opportunity to live in response to God's love."

—REV. JOSEPH V. CROCKETT
Special Assistance to the President, American Bible Society

D0829419

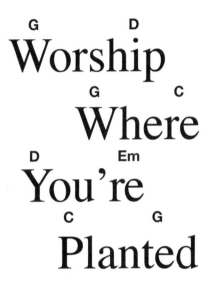

Worship Where You're Planted

A Primer for the Local Church Worship Leader

DAVE CLARK

BEACON HILL PRESS
OF KANSAS CITY

Copyright 2010
by Dave Clark and Beacon Hill Press of Kansas City

ISBN 978-0-8341-2555-1

Printed in the
United States of America

Cover Design: Brandon Hill
Internal Design: Sharon Page

Library of Congress Cataloging-in-Publication Data

Clark, Dave.
    Worship where you're planted : a primer for the local church worship leader / Dave
Clark.
        p. cm.
    ISBN 978-0-8341-2555-1 (pbk.)
    1. Church music. 2. Public worship. I. Title.
    ML3001.C56 2010
    264'.2—dc22

                                                                      2010023980

10 9 8 7 6 5 4 3 2 1

Contents

Acknowledgments

I have spent a lifetime chasing moments. Along the way God has allowed me to encounter some incredible people who have led me, loved me, and left me a better person in the process. It is to them I dedicate this book with my deepest thanks.

Rev. Daryl Blank and my family at Goodlettsville Tennessee, Church of the Nazarene.

Dr. Bob Broadbooks and Dr. Gary Henecke, who continue to mentor me.

Ed Hogan, Eric Cornell, Keith Sealy, and Donna Goodrich, who brought so much to this project.

Emily Higinbotham—what started as a part-time job God has transformed into a full-time ministry. I could not do it without you.

Tim Curtis and all my NPH family for pausing to listen to the song God has given me.

My parents, Orville and Louise Clark, who raised me in an atmosphere where I would know God's voice when I heard it. The music you taught me is alive and well.

And especially to my wife, Cindi, who continues to teach me that home is more than where I live. To Allison, Anna, and Sam, who fill these rooms with life. I am blessed.

Introduction

When we first discussed the possibility of a resource book for worship leaders of small to mid-size churches, I had mixed emotions. While these are the churches I have spent the majority of my years with and where my heart remains, I wasn't sure I was the one to write it.

In the interest of full disclosure, I should say up front that I don't read many books or go to many conferences dealing with the topic of leading worship. I have never been comfortable with the idea of those who don't know me telling me how I should lead worship at a church they've never attended. Since they don't know our geography or people and have never worked with our soloists or musicians, how could they possibly have a sense for what style of music works for us? The obvious question then becomes, *Why would I set out to write a book intended to accomplish something I have already said I don't think is possible?*

The reason I accepted this assignment is that even though our situations are unique and require specific solutions, I believe for many of us the struggles we face are common ones. Few would dispute the fact that these are difficult days for many worship leaders. We are being led or driven toward a musical identity crisis whether we are ready for it or not. There is the constant pressure to adapt to the current trends of music style, technology that seems to change by the hour, and congregations who are increasingly more vocal in their opinions. Somewhere in the middle of it all, if you are like me, you struggle to find the balance between who and what God called us to be and the constantly changing demands of ministry.

As we collectively learn to navigate through these new and uncharted waters, we find that everyone gets there in a different way. Some prefer the safety of isolationism, building the walls high and sturdy enough to prevent the pain from inflicting any permanent damage. Others tend to dig their heels in, ready for battle, only to find themselves listed among the wounded. When things are going well, I am convinced there is no place more rewarding to serve than on a church platform on a Sunday morning. Unfortunately, I don't have to remind you that the opposite is also true. During those times when simple encouragement is a scarce commodity, we all need to be reminded that we are not the first—nor the only ones—to feel this way.

In researching this project, I sent out questionnaires to both male and female worship leaders representing different denominations, different regions of the country, and different age groups. What I learned was not so much a surprise as it was a confirmation of what I already suspected: What unites us is far greater than what separates us. From the fears and frustrations to the seasons of blessings, we all share in and continue to learn from each other. In fact, the very premise of this book is that we might recognize, analyze, react, and respond to the situations and solutions that each of us encounters from Sunday to Sunday.

[1] Here I Am to Worship

*You're new at the church, and the worship leader you are
replacing holds a place next to sainthood in the hearts of
the people. He retired from leading but chose to stay at the
church. He is free with his opinions and not shy about his
influence. He offers his insight and assistance to you as long
as you agree with him.*

Not too long after I began my first assignment as a worship
leader, a friend offered some powerful insight I found more
valid with each passing year. He said, "There is no difference
between a large church and a small church when it comes to
how hard you work." He went on to explain that in a large
church, while there are more responsibilities, there is usually
a larger staff and many more people to share the responsibilities, so the workload is essentially the same.

When I look back at some of the lessons I learned over
the next few years, I realize he could have added some other
things as well. He could have told me the only thing part-time
about a part-time staff position is the salary, because most
of the time people will have full-time expectations. Maybe
he could have warned me how the church would always take
as much as I was willing to give or discouraged me with the
grim reminder that at any given moment someone would not
agree with what I was doing or how I was doing my job.

Would this advice have mattered? Most assuredly not,
because I was confident that what I lacked in experience and
technique I could more than compensate for with optimism,
creativity, and a good work ethic. Add to that a peace in my
spirit, which could have come only by knowing God's Spirit

was at work in my heart, and off I went. That should have been enough. Right?

I soon discovered one thing the church has in common with politics is what is known as the "honeymoon period." If this phrase appeared in the dictionary, it would read like this:

honeymoon period |ˈhənēˌmoōn' pi(ə)rēəd|

noun—*a length or portion of time when people celebrate your arrival even as they begin to speculate on your departure. Duration is flexible and at the sole discretion of anyone who has an opinion on said matter. On or before completion of this term, any previous attempts at decorum are no longer needed.*

That may be a little harsh and somewhat cynical, yet it is nonetheless all too often real. I remember asking my wife, who grew up in a parsonage, if this was just a music thing or if my parents had protected me from this kind of stuff while I was growing up. Her reply was "No and yes."

I heard someone say once that you cannot teach until those you are teaching trust. It is therefore crucial during this honeymoon period for you to build up as much trust equity with the people as possible. Don't be afraid to go where they are and embrace them. Appeal to their hearts before you try to appeal to their intellect. Get your hands dirty. Let them know you came not only to lead but also to walk with them. I have always found that as important as it is for followers to know their leaders, it is even more important for leaders to know their followers.

First impressions, whether positive or negative, tend to last a long time. On some level you have to operate under the assumption that if the previous program worked, you probably would not be there, so don't be afraid to take your followers to some new places. It is equally important to remember that you cannot lead people *to* this new place unless you have a good idea where you are leading them *from*. Sometimes this comes from asking questions, other times from simple observation. You can be assured that when you ask an opinion you will always get one; so bear in mind that it is just that—one opinion. In other words, if you don't want to know, don't ask.

I remember a young worship pastor telling me about his new assignment. He said he couldn't wait to get there and rock their world and show them how to worship. As you might imagine, his tenure at that church did not last nearly as long as he expected.

Choir room bookshelves and old orders of worship also offer great insight. If a choir book is too worn out, it was probably used too often. If it looks brand new, there may be a reason why it was not used. I will address the hymns-versus-choruses debate in a later chapter, but it is important to know the landscape of where the church has been musically. What you discover may or may not determine your direction, but if nothing else, it will help prepare you for the people's reaction.

Something else to remember when it comes to the small to mid-size congregation is that these are traditionally the churches where change comes most slowly. I have even heard of situations where people felt obligated to hold on to past musical styles or traditions out of some perceived loyalty to a deceased relative. In a larger church, those two or three families make up a very small percentage of the whole. But in

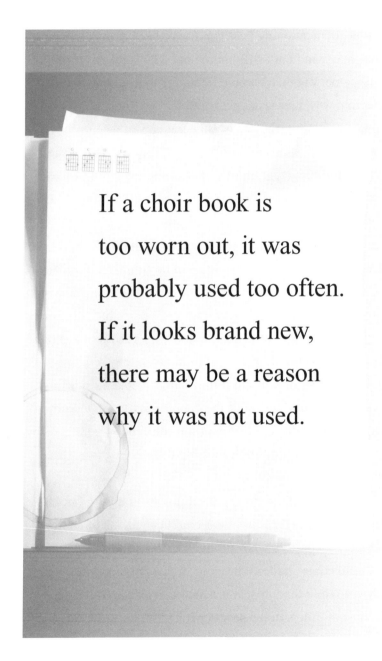

If a choir book is
too worn out, it was
probably used too often.
If it looks brand new,
there may be a reason
why it was not used.

a small church, a few families can easily represent the majority. It bears mentioning here that I have been at my church for seven years, and I am still finding out who is related to whom. In the same way that it would be wrong to discount everything that was, it is as dangerous to try to mimic the footsteps you inherited. Yes, the pastor encouraged you when you were hired to bring vision and implement change. Yes, he or she told you the congregation was ready to be more progressive musically. No, he or she didn't mean to do it all at once starting on your first Sunday.

If you are presently serving a church, it is safe to say you have already discovered that you will be compared both positively and negatively with the previous worship leader. In my situation it was extremely rare that not just one but two former worship leaders still attended the church. Even rarer was that, unlike the opening scenario in this chapter, they remained my biggest supporters, and if they had personal agendas, I never saw them. If you have the opportunity to get to know the previous leader, most of the time you can do more good by acknowledging his or her leadership than feeling threatened by it.

After I had been at the church for about a year, our choir was preparing to do a live recording. I called one of the former worship pastors who still lived in town and asked him if he would come and lead the choir in prayer before the evening service. While the intent was genuine, it also accomplished a couple of things in the process. It let him know he was still very much loved by the choir, and it gave me a chance to thank him for his part in preparing the way for where God was leading. I should also admit that I thoroughly enjoyed watching the surprise on the choir members' faces.

Somewhere along the way I fear we—meaning the Church—have lost the art of good transition. We tend to primarily use this word when we are leaving a situation, but I believe how we transition *in* can go a long way toward setting the tone for the day we transition *out.*

The Promise: "God has made us sufficient ministers of the new covenant, not of the letter but of the Spirit, for the letter kills, but the Spirit gives life" (2 Corinthians 3:6, NKJV).

The Prayer: *Lord, you know my desire is to have a heart after you. Cleanse this temple where you have called me to serve, and cleanse this temple of my heart as I daily lay it at your feet.*

Contemplation Questions

1. What was your biggest surprise between the interview and the first six months?

2. If you could go back and change the first impression of you, what would you change?

3. What did the church do right during the transition?

4. What would you change if you were senior pastor?

5. What are you doing to build some trust equity in the short term? In the long term?

2

Holy Tension

Nancy plays the piano. She played the piano before you came and has let it be known she intends to play long after you're gone. Her mother played the piano before her, and everyone knows that. She cannot play the new styles of worship and has made it painfully clear that she will not step down voluntarily.

On the list of things referred to as sacred in many churches is a *cow*. No one really knows how long the cow has been sacred; it just has. Down through the years I have seen this sacred cow take on a variety of shapes, including everything from a handbell to a hymnal and a pulpit to a pew. I have also discovered the most dangerous variety of sacred cow is the one you're unaware is sacred to begin with. In fact, years can pass without your ever realizing the significance it holds—or the passion it can inspire.

I deeply regret that in far too many churches over the past decade or so, music has found its way onto this list. How sad that what was intended to bring us together, united in praise before a holy God, has somehow become a catalyst of division! I remember the early days of what was unfortunately deemed the *worship wars*—the dissension over singing from the hymnal versus singing some of the newer choruses. But now it seems this sacred cow has expanded its territory into greener pastures. In many cases, it is no longer enough to debate the style of the music—now we have also added the instruments being played and the proper attire of those playing them.

I want to go out on a bit of a limb here and suggest something I do not hear much about. There is a long-held assumption that the tension regarding music is something that exists between the worship leader and the congregation. My fear is that in just as many situations, the tension of worship style rests between the worship leader and the senior pastor.

Let me try to explain my basis for this assertion. See if this sounds familiar: Your church is not big enough to pay you a full-time salary, so you work a regular job during the week in order to support your family and your love for music. You are somewhere between thirty and forty years old, and you have been at the church for at least ten years through at least two pastors. Relocation is not really an option, because your family is settled and the kids like their school. The people in the congregation are among your closest friends. Just when you think everything is going great, the pastor informs you that he or she feels that the music is stagnant and is keeping the church from growing like the church down the street.

How do I know so much about you? It is because you are part of a large and rapidly increasing demographic of worship leaders in small to mid-size churches who are faced with an uncomfortable dilemma. You can try to lead a style of music that is neither your passion nor your strength, or you can step aside from the very thing that brings you the greatest joy and sense of purpose in ministry. The pressure is high, and the options are few. There are very few other churches in the area and, even if there were, there is a good chance they have already made the move toward a more contemporary style of worship. So, like many others faced with the same predicament, you convince yourself that it is better to lead what you think is expected and, in the process, lay aside the instincts that have led you through the years.

Is it wrong for the pastor to make such a request? Honestly, there is probably something inside all of us at times that would love to challenge pastors on the same point. Are they adapting their preaching style as well, or are they placing the entire burden for growth on the shoulders of the worship leader?

Since that approach will almost certainly lead you from the platform to the pew, let's look at some other options. Rather than fear the changing dynamic, I encourage you to remember that you are a worship leader. You do not have to forfeit your dreams or your call, just your mind-set. How long has it been since you honestly challenged yourself? This is never easy and usually comes with growing pains. Don't forget that this is also a new journey for those you are leading.

What concerns me most is that somewhere along the way we have shifted the discussion to style of music when it should be about quality of content. Even more important is asking yourself whether or not you are allowing the Spirit to move you through new music. While a question like that will surely cause some to bristle, it is still one you must ask yourself. In fact, here are a few other questions I would add to the list.

1. Do you regularly listen to new styles of worship music as a part of your personal devotions?

2. Are you quicker to dismiss a certain song because you assume your congregation will not like it?

3. Deep down inside do you worry that if you open the door to a new style you may never get it closed again?

There will always be those on the fringe of both sides who claim to speak for many yet represent few or, as I call them, the five-percent majority.

While it is all well and good to view yourself as a gate-keeper of tradition, tradition alone is by its very nature merely passing along what was handed to you. Is that really compelling enough to sustain you in ministry? Several years ago a friend of mine and I wrote a song we knew would never get recorded, but we went ahead and wrote it anyway. The chorus went something like this: "Don't give me that old-time religion. I want something fresh and new. Reminding me that you're still Lord of all I'm going through." How current is your relationship with the Lord? What did He teach you today?

When I was still leading worship, I was not overly concerned with whether the music style was labeled progressive or traditional. For some it may have pushed the envelope a little, while the same songs for others may have been too conservative. There will always be those on the fringe of both sides who claim to speak for many yet represent few or, as I call them, the five-percent majority. As you have already discovered, you will not please this five percent no matter what you do. These are normally the same people who also feel compelled to complain about the length of the sermon as well as the look of the bulletin. One of the biggest mistakes I made early on was to try to accommodate the fringe.

It has been my experience that many churches are filled with people who would be shocked to know that people are complaining at all. In my case, I eventually resorted to one simple sentence that seemed to disarm most of the complaints. I responded, "You may be surprised if I were to lead by my personal preferences." Because they were not totally sure what that meant, they usually turned and walked away, and I continued to lead as God led me.

If you will allow me to digress a little from the topic of the sacred cows, I feel this may be an appropriate place to interject my personal preferences about style of worship music. I realize, first of all, that they are just that—personal preferences. Because I was raised with a hymnal in my hands yet have spent most of my life writing new songs, it gives me somewhat of a unique perspective. I absolutely love the level of craft represented in the hymns. I also would consider it a travesty for my generation to be so arrogant as to decide that songs that in some cases have lived for over two hundred years are no longer good enough or relevant for today. I remember hearing Gloria Gaither say, "We don't do the old songs because they are old—we do them because they are good." If you want an example of a great praise and worship song, take a look at the old hymn "Immortal, Invisible." Both musically and lyrically, it is a virtual clinic in how to write a song.

I also love many of the new songs. I just prefer the ones that are written with the same level of craft. Just because it is high on the CCLI charts does not alone make it a good song. At some point it comes down to what musical setting you put the song in. If your congregation leans toward the new choruses and you miss the hymns, the marketplace offers many newer treatments of old texts. A songwriter friend in Iowa did not grow up with the hymnal as I did. After her husband bought her one a few years ago as a gift, she went through and picked out the lyrics that moved her and set them to beautiful melodies.

My point is that it does not have to be one or the other. It just has to be authentic. You know your congregation, and assuming you have earned their trust to lead them, then, as Nike says, "Just do it."

If you have led worship for more than one month, I suspect you have already encountered the human variety of sacred cows. They are usually easy to spot, because they go out of the way to make you know who they are, and they must be handled very delicately. At one church I attended, "Catherine" was a self-appointed matriarch of the choir, the special music, and all things musical. If she came to choir practice, she informed you how long she had been in the choir and whether or not she liked a particular song, as if one had any bearing on the other. If she chose to not sing on Sunday, I could almost feel the choir watching her for approval rather than worshiping. If someone brought it up, invariably the response would be "Well, that's just Catherine."

Initially I tried to win her over, but I quickly found myself falling into the same trap as those who had been there a long time. I knew it would be hard to break the cycle of appeasement, yet I was determined that it had to be done. I began to shift the dialog with her away from music. I stopped asking where she was when she was not at choir practice, but I did ask about her family and continued to invest myself in her life through other avenues. When a storm blew down trees in her yard, I borrowed a chainsaw and went to work. When she got sick and needed prayer, I was there. She and I never did get to the same page when it came to music, but we found a different foundation on which to build trust, and we began to get along fine. It wasn't long before the choir began to follow the same pattern. The lesson I learned was that when I stopped allowing her to set the tempo, it was amazing how the others stopped following.

What are the sacred cows at your church? Is it the organ that no one plays or hymnals that seldom get used? Is it the singer who always gets the solo or a matter of who stands where in the choir? I don't know anyone who enjoys being the heavy when it comes to addressing longstanding issues such as these, but many times it has to be done if the church is to go where God wants to lead it. Make sure, however, that the Lord has your heart and the pastor has your back before and as you move forward. Be consistent in your method and bathe the process in prayer. Keep decisions from becoming personal, and remember that change is seldom easy for anyone, but if there is tension, no one wins.

The Promise: "In all thy ways acknowledge him, and he shall direct thy paths" (Proverbs 3:6, KJV).

The Prayer: *Dear Lord, shine your light on me and reveal your ways to me. Give me the words to say and the wisdom not to get ahead of you. Most of all, Lord, I pray that you will direct my paths.*

Contemplation Questions

1. How long did it take you to discover your first sacred cow?

2. Does the music you are leading reflect your personal tastes or the preferences of someone else?

3. How healthy is the dialog between you and your pastor? What are you doing to improve it?

4. When you feel the stress of tension, do you internalize it or share it with those you trust?

5. How often do you think about what else you would do if you were not leading worship?

3

Preaching
to the Choir

You have too many singers for a praise team, yet not enough for a choir. You have experimented with singing a special once a month instead of every Sunday. Some of your people look at the choir as a place to serve, while others view it as just another commitment.

In the small Michigan town where I grew up, choir was a regular part of every church service. About thirty-five people dressed in gray robes complete with reversible stoles. I know they were reversible, because on Christmas and Easter they were always turned inside out.

Looking back, I'm not sure how the choir was able to function at all. Think about it. There were no specialized microphones or dedicated track lighting. Floor monitors were not needed, because there was no such thing as a soundtrack. There were no screens with the words, and if there were solos, I don't remember them. A name like John W. Peterson on a cantata cover was enough to ensure sales, and it was okay to do the same cantata two years in a row. It amazes me how much choir has evolved over the last fifty years.

Or has it?

In the name of progress we have changed almost every-thing about choir except the choir itself. It still comes down to a group of nonprofessional volunteers who enjoy singing. In many cases, especially in the small church, it is not man-datory to read music or sing on pitch. The only qualification for being a member of the choir usually amounts to merely showing up, and the size of the group seldom rises above ten percent of the congregation.

If you do not currently have a choir in your church, you might be tempted to skip over these next few chapters. Some of you might even be tempted to skip them because you *do* have a choir. I want to go on record as saying I do not pretend to be an authority on choirs or choir practices. Even so, I have some strong feelings about the choir and the place it can hold in a worship service, no matter the size of the church. When I hear people talk about choir as no longer being relevant in today's culture, I am always curious as to what series of events led them to this conclusion.

Much to my regret, I have heard of too many situations in recent years where rather than improve what is no longer working, the choice is made to simply discontinue the choir altogether. I know the analogy is a little over the top, but to me it is like getting rid of the piano because it needs tuning. Before you do something drastic, let's talk about some possible ways to tune the choir up a little.

Because a later chapter will deal with choir rehearsal vocal techniques, I will skip over that for now, but I do want to talk about the rehearsal itself. I am assuming that hidden somewhere in Scripture is a specific mandate that choir rehearsal can be held only Wednesday evenings, or Sunday afternoons for those of you who still have Sunday evening service. At my church I inherited the traditional Wednesday evening time slot. I had not been there very long before I began to notice some definite trends.

1. There were a handful of the same people who always seemed to show up early.

My first lesson: Don't save last-minute preparation till the last minute.

2. There were a handful of the same people who always seemed to show up late.

My second lesson: If I wait till everyone is there, we will never get started.

3. There were a handful of the same people who always seemed to have all the questions.

My third lesson: There are a handful of the same people who always seem to have all the answers.

I think you get my point. Old habits die hard, and in my situation, it seemed they all found their resting place in the choir room on Wednesday nights. I should also add that just as the choir members came in with their preconceived notions about what choir should look and sound like, I also came armed with my own laundry list of personal pet peeves regarding choir.

For example, I love choir books—but only on Wednesdays. I have always been fascinated with ministers of music who complain about people looking down at a hymnal during congregational worship yet have no problem with their choir looking down at a choir book during the special music. To me, it is almost the same thing, except a choir is actually ministering to the congregation. I agree that this is a much more viable option when there is a screen on the back wall with the lyrics, but even that is not a necessity.

Is the choir going to sing the wrong notes periodically? *Of course they are.* Will it have a negative impact on the service if they do? *I have never seen it happen.* I base this

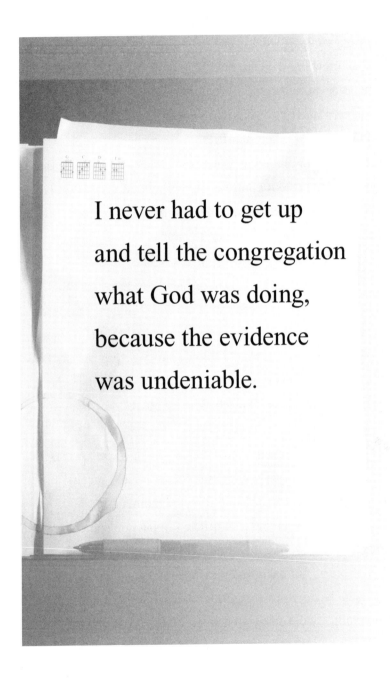

I never had to get up
and tell the congregation
what God was doing,
because the evidence
was undeniable.

on a belief that even though we strive for a technically perfect performance, we do not sing to perfect listeners. Every Sunday morning the church is filled with ordinary people who bring hurts and struggles through the doors and need to be ministered to. They may listen with their ears, but they react and respond with their hearts.

As you can imagine, it was somewhat of a struggle the first time I asked our choir to sing without books on Sunday, and it was not an immediate success. In the long run, however, a sense of freedom began to happen on the platform because the choir was not bound to a book.

Another of my long-term goals was to transform the choir room into a safe zone on Wednesday nights. This, too, is not an overnight process and requires a level of trust that has to be earned over time. I know some worship leaders who believe choir practice is—well, a time only to practice choir music. I know others who schedule a time for devotions at the close of each rehearsal.

I would not presume to say one way or the other is right or wrong or better or worse. I seldom planned a specific time for devotions but learned to follow the moment. If I felt a particular song was having a significant impact on someone, I did not hesitate to stop in the middle of the song and talk about it. It also was not uncommon to spontaneously begin singing a prayer chorus if it felt right. It comes down to a matter of leadership style. I found that when I led with sensitivity and vulnerability, it let the choir know it was okay to be vulnerable before God and with each other.

What I began to see develop was a group of people investing in each other's lives in a powerful way. The moving of God on Wednesday nights began to have a direct overflow into the Sunday morning service. I never had to get up and tell the congregation what God was doing, because the evidence was undeniable. Week in and week out, I watched this small group of reckless worshipers being used of God in a mighty way. One lady's husband pastored a small nearby church. Because of that, she couldn't sing with us on Sundays, but she never missed a Wednesday night rehearsal. It was fascinating that the less we focused on the performance, the more effective the choir special became as a part of worship. That is the kind of choir I want to be a part of.

In spite of how little emphasis I placed on the performance, I am a huge student of good communication. I wrestle constantly with the question of how we get what is in our hearts to connect with that person on the second row. Is louder volume better than softer volume? Does the congregation respond better to up-tempo songs or ballads? Should the choir special come before or after the offering? Does a video on the screen distract from or accentuate the choir song? It is a never-ending pursuit that completely intrigues me. Because of that, I have discovered that distractions that seem minor to most people are major ones to me.

My pastor and I spend a lot of time analyzing everything about the service as we try to pinpoint what works and what does not. We challenge each other with tough questions on how to improve the delivery, and both of us admit we enjoy the ongoing dialog. In fact, he kids me that he can't enjoy anything as much as he used to before he met me because he is watching too closely now. If I did not believe it mattered, I would not work nearly as hard on trying to improve it.

Back in the early eighties I traveled for five years as a guitar player with a group called The Speer Family. They were my favorite gospel group as a kid, and I felt blessed to be a part of their ministry for those years. One Sunday morning we held a concert at the Nazarene church in Alexandria, Indiana. If the name of the town sounds familiar, it is because of a songwriter named Bill Gaither who invited the world into his backyard through his music and videos.

As an aspiring songwriter myself, you can probably imagine how intimidated I was that morning when Bill and Gloria walked in and sat down. After the service, Gloria came up to me and asked why I didn't smile more. At a complete loss for words, I mumbled something about just being the guitar player and how no one came to see me anyway. I still remember her response. "When it comes to communication," she said, "everyone has to be involved." She went on to say that no one is more or less important than anyone else. After I got over the fact—and the thrill—of being lectured by a legend, I began to think about what she said. In the remaining years with the group, I never had to be told again to smile.

Why do I share that story here? It's because another troubling issue for me when it comes to choir is to watch part of the group completely involved in the song while a few others appear to be completely disengaged. We will discuss in another chapter some ideas on how to invest the choir in the song so that it becomes personal for each of them, but for now

I want to address the issue of platform distractions. I have a philosophy I am pretty sure is different from most choir directors. If there is someone in the choir who is less than one-hundred-percent on board with the special of the week, I would rather he or she sit out in the congregation that Sunday. When it comes to communicating the song, I much prefer a smaller choir with everyone involved in the song than to have every seat full yet not everyone committed.

Are distractions going on with your choir that diminishes its effectiveness? Almost certainly there are. If not, you are in a very rare situation. The bigger the choir, the greater the chance for distraction. Because every church is different, the easiest way to evaluate your choir's performance is to set up a video camera in the back of the church. Record the presentation for several weeks, and don't be afraid to make an honest assessment.

Watch for things such as the entrance and exit of the choir. One of the most disruptive events in a service is when the choir finishes its song. Is there a smoother or less disruptive way to come off the platform? Does the choir exit through a side door? If so, do they then go into a room to take off their robes, only to interrupt the service again five minutes later when they re-enter the sanctuary and sit down? If the song has a solo part, does the singer come out and wait through the whole introduction of the song before singing? After the solo is done, does he or she take the seat on the end of a row or walk past five people in the second row simply because that is where he or she always stands? You can easily remedy another visual distraction by arranging people by height.

It is time well spent to set aside part of a rehearsal, show the video to the choir members, and open up dialog with them about the need for better communication. These suggestions are only a jumping-off point, but I hope they'll encourage you to come up with your own list.

The Promise: "You will be his witness to all men of what you have seen and heard" (Acts 22:15, NIV).

The Prayer: *Lord, I pray that our voices will make a difference in the lives of many for your sake.*

Contemplation Questions

1. How long has it been since you did an honest assessment of your choir?

2. Do you believe in the concept of choir as strongly as you once did?

3. How do you think people in the congregation perceive the choir?

4. Is your choir driven by routine or by passion?

5. Do you have a choir simply because there has always been a choir?

6. What kind of impact does your choir have on the worship service?

4

Investment
Strategies

You're starting to feel less like a worship leader and more like a motivational speaker. No matter how much you talk about level of dedication, it does not seem to matter. From choir practice to congregational singing, sometimes you wonder if people are as committed as they used to be.

Those who know me know that I can relate almost any situation to an old episode of the *Andy Griffith Show*. One of my favorites is called "Andy Discovers America," which first aired in 1963. In this particular episode, Opie's teacher, Miss Crump, is trying without success to get her students excited about American history. Just when she is so frustrated she is about to quit teaching altogether, Andy gets involved and tells the boys the same story in a different way. The next day at school, Opie and his friends can't wait to rattle off dates and places as if they have known the information for years. Needless to say, Miss Crump is blindsided by the sudden change in their attitudes and goes directly to the sheriff's office to discover Andy's secret. It turns out that Andy doesn't have a hidden formula guaranteed to get the boys interested; rather, he used what I refer to as a good investment strategy. He did not change the story at all; he just found a way to invest the listener in what he was saying.

I heard another example of this technique from a mother whose little boy was entering his first season of Little League baseball. She went to the introductory meeting with the other parents, expecting a list of mandatory practices and unexpected costs. Instead, the coach began telling stories about young men who had come through the baseball program in years past and the positive lifelong effects it had on them. Rather than adding more things to the parents' to-do lists, he spent the time investing them in the game of baseball. As he passed around the commitment sign-up sheet, this mother could hardly wait to add her name to the list—all because a coach came prepared with a good investment strategy.

Of all the ideas covered in this book, I have been most anxious to write about this concept, as I am convinced it has the greatest potential for immediate and long-term impact. It is more than just a device intended to get more response from your choir or congregation. In fact, I would go so far as to say that if you try to implement the concepts of this chapter with this secondary motivation, not only will it not work, but it also stands a good chance of diminishing your credibility as a leader. Why do I believe that? Because at the very core of a good investment strategy is *authenticity*.

Allow me a point of redundancy by stating the obvious: You cannot invest your people in something you do not completely believe in yourself. For example, have you ever tried to teach your choir or congregation a new song only because the pastor asked you to? It may not be wrong to do a song for that reason; however, it is important for you to invest yourself in the song first. Find a part of the song that moves you—the melody, lyric, or even the arrangement—and use that as a point of focus as you lead it. I remember one song that I really did not get, but it had such an impact on one of the choir members that I found myself drawn to it for that reason alone. In most cases, if there were not some positive quality in the song, it wouldn't have found its way into your hands to begin with. Always trust what moves you as a barometer of a good song, but know your followers well enough to trust what moves them as well.

In one church, the money was tight and the ensuing spending freeze started with no new choir music. A year later, the minister of music encouraged the choir members to buy their own books. Obviously, that particular book was each member's favorite of all the books on the shelf. While that is one way to get a choir invested in the music, it would be tough to sustain a music program with that technique alone. Let's talk about other, more practical, investment strategies starting with the choir.

Whatever the size of the choir, there is bound to be a cross-section of ages as well as musical style preferences. As most songwriters have discovered, there are many different levels of listening. Some people are naturally drawn to the lyrical content, while others react to the rhythm or the sound of the instrumentation. So how does a leader invest such a diverse group into one vision? The answer is that you do not. What you can do, however, is train them to find a place to tie into the song.

Let me give you an example: It was a fairly common occurrence in rehearsal that if I felt the singing on a particular song lacked excitement, I stopped in the middle of it, called out someone who seemed to be completely into the song, and asked the person what a certain line meant to him or her personally. More often than not, the choir member would offer something I had not thought of at all. I would then pose the same question to another person who seemed somewhat disengaged from the song. That investment strategy usually accomplished two things. First, it challenged others in the choir to examine what the line meant to them, and second, it served as a reminder to all the choir members in the room to be on their toes in case I called on them.

I also asked other questions from time to time such as "Why do you think the melody lifted on a certain phrase?" or, "If you close your eyes when you sing this, what picture do you see? Do you see it in color?"

One of my favorite tactics was to pick out a line or a phrase and ask the choir how they would have written it if they were the writer. As they began to put the lyrics into their own words, they were investing themselves into the very heart of the song. I was always intrigued with the responses I heard. I was also amazed by how much better they sang when we returned to the original lyric. A note of caution: do not use this technique unless you have first asked yourself the same questions. What does the song mean to *you*? What drew *you* to it to begin with?

Another investment strategy is to offer real-life applications to the theme of the song. If the song we were rehearsing dealt with the topic of God's grace through pain, I would encourage someone who had been in that situation to share with the others what God had taught him or her about grace. If the song was about joy, we would stop and praise the Lord. I don't remember a single time when the song lost momentum by stopping in the middle of it for a discussion. Without exception, I found the opposite to be true.

In my situation, because many of the writers of the songs we used were friends of mine, it was not uncommon for me to share something in the writer's life that may have played a part in how or why the song was written. You may be thinking, *That's nice for him, but how does that help me?* With the fingertip accessibility of the Internet, you would be amazed at the information available. Many writers have their own sites, and publishers may often include a short bio on the writer as well.

One song our choir loved was "Days of Elijah." They sang it loudly and with big smiles. One night in the middle of rehearsal I asked if anyone knew what the song was about. One person offered a reasonable explanation. I then pointed to another line and asked how that line tied in to the explanation. After a great deal of discussion, I picked up a printout from the songwriter's web site where she explained what was behind the writing of the song. That may seem like a lot of wasted time for a song they already liked, but I assure you that the destination was more than worth the journey. The difference between merely singing words and music and a group of singers being completely invested in a song may very well be the difference between a listener simply hearing a song and being transformed by it.

Investment strategies for your congregation are every bit as important as the ones used with your choir, yet they require a much different approach on your part. I will discuss this in two different sections. In the first section, I want to deal with songs already familiar to the congregation, then discuss possible options for investing them in songs that are brand new.

One of the more fascinating memories I have of the church I grew up in was that we ended every service by sing-

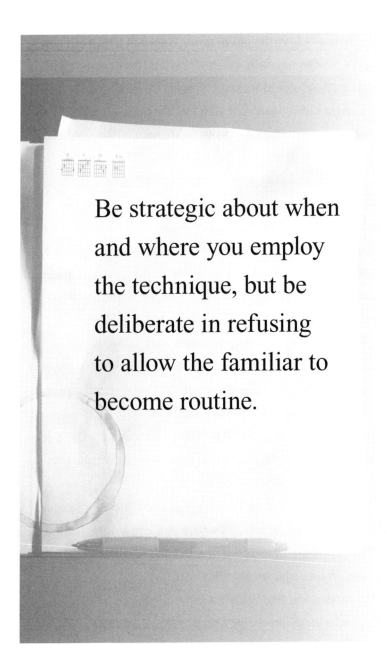

Be strategic about when and where you employ the technique, but be deliberate in refusing to allow the familiar to become routine.

ing the Doxology. Now don't get me wrong—I have already told you how I love the old hymns. Yet years later I am still curious how words such as "Praise God, from whom all blessings flow" could be sung with all the passion of a funeral dirge. As a kid, I wondered if the music minister was intentionally trying to stretch out the final amen of the song to keep us there longer. It was not the song's fault, however. The lyrics are majestic, and the music itself still invokes an attitude of praise. So what was the problem? The congregation either was never invested in the song or somewhere along the way had grown comfortable with the words. Down through the years, some of the least inspiring worship I have heard comes from sincere people in the habit of singing a familiar song in a familiar way.

Many times the solution is as simple as breaking the pattern. If we had known the story behind the Doxology, that it was originally the final stanza of the twelve-verse hymn "Awake, My Soul, and with the Sun," would it have mattered? What if just once the song had been placed at a different point in the service or led by someone other than the music minister?

I'm not advocating breaking the pattern every Sunday. Be strategic about when and where you employ the technique, but be deliberate in refusing to allow the familiar to become routine. While a larger church might have the musicians try a different musical feel behind a familiar song, you may find the solution to breaking the pattern as easy as not using instruments for a verse—or even an entire service. How long has it been since you shared a story behind a song or told how a song has impacted you? Only you know your patterns and how best to break them.

If the investment strategy for a familiar song relies on breaking the pattern, a new song relies on the power of the first impression. Over the past few months I have seen two completely different examples that brought this point home to me. In one case the minister of music wanted to teach the congregation a new song. Rather than simply add it to the order of worship and act as if everyone should already know it, he used it to close the service. Not coincidentally, it dovetailed perfectly with the pastor's sermon. The first time through, it was sung as a solo and then the congregation was invited to join in the second time. Because of the strategic placement, it quickly became a favorite of the congregation.

The second example happened on a Sunday morning when a visiting minister of music decided to teach the congregation three new songs at one time. Needless to say, worship was not very inclusive in that service. I would rather hear the same chorus used three weeks in a row than to get three weeks worth of it on one Sunday. Forcing a song, no matter what the style, is not an effective investment strategy. If it is a new song, why did you choose it? Does it go along with the theme of the service, or do you simply like how it feels when you sing it?

It would be easy after reading this chapter to conclude that I am telling you to talk a lot in order to invest people in the song. That is not the case at all. Let the preacher preach. You were hired to lead worship. Words are only one way to get there.

I began this chapter talking about authenticity, and I want to close the chapter the same way. No matter what strategies you use, they have to reflect your strengths and personality in order to be effective. What worked for me may not work for you, but the concept is definitely worth pursuing.

The Promise: "For God so loved the world, that he gave his only begotten Son, that whosoever believeth in him should not perish, but have everlasting life" (John 3:16, KJV).

The Prayer: *Lord, you have invested in me your only Son. How can I offer anything less in return?*

Contemplation Questions

1. How convinced are you of what you are trying to convince them of?

2. How long has it been since you tried a brand-new approach to leading?

3. Are you allowing your church to invest in you?

4. Do you trust your sense of awareness of whether or not they are following what you are leading?

5. What is your gauge for measuring the level of investment return?

5

Every
Seven Days

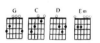

You would prefer to build the order of worship around the pastor's message. The problem is you really want to prepare several weeks ahead, and your pastor normally doesn't finish the sermon until a week ahead. It is hard to be accountable to a schedule over which you have no control.

No matter the size of the church, worship leaders are unique individuals. The very nature of the job requires the ability to successfully navigate between both the right and the left sides of the brain during any given week. The demands these leaders face are diverse, running the gamut from strict in the area of tempo to flexibility when it comes to musical interpretation. They must be able to relate to a church board yet know how to communicate with a volunteer drummer. They listen to Christmas musicals in the summer, Easter musicals in the winter, and usually have at least one manger in their garage at home. Another peculiarity is the way they talk with other worship leaders. They use phrases such as "Easter comes early this year" or "Christmas comes on Sunday."

If I could coin a phrase based on one of the most important lessons I learned as a worship leader, it would be something to the effect of "Sunday comes every seven days." It is an especially poignant reality check for those of you who are bi-vocational. It does not matter how valid your distractions are throughout the week; Sunday still comes every seven days.

Once the service starts, the seats will be filled with young people, old people, saints, seekers, and worshipers. Some come searching for fellowship, while others walk through the doors carrying burdens too deep to share with

Every Sunday holds
the potential to be a
red-letter day in
someone's spiritual
journey, and music may
very well be the impetus
God uses.

anyone. They probably don't care what kind of week you've had; they're just hoping and praying that the music you've prepared meets their expectations. Every Sunday holds the potential to be a red-letter day in someone's spiritual journey, and music may very well be the impetus God uses. No one could blame you if somewhere in the middle of planning the worship order you find yourself staring at a blank page slightly intimidated by the reminder that Sunday comes every seven days.

I am probably safe in assuming that if you are reading this book, you already have some tried-and-true systems in place for preparing an order of worship. Even so, since one of the goals of this book is to encourage you to break some patterns, I hope you will stick with me for these next few pages.

When I first began as a worship leader, I received a lot of good advice from other ministers of music. One not-so-good tidbit, however, came from a well-meaning friend who told me that a part-time music position at a church really did not require that much time. He suggested I come up with seven or eight orders of worship and rotate them every month or so. I refer to this as bad advice—not because I tried it and it didn't work, but rather because I knew even then that there was too much at stake to rely on such a simplistic approach.

One thing that surprised me most in my own unofficial survey was how many senior pastors actually provide the minister of music with the order of worship. If that is your situation, I am tempted to offer my condolences, because you are missing out on one of the most rewarding parts of the process. The payoff for me was getting to stand on the platform every Sunday morning and experience the ordination of the hour at the intersection of my reliance and God's revelation. I literally could hardly wait each week to see what God was going to do through a sequence of songs He had already played a huge part in. Time after time after time, I could see His hand at work in seasons and situations I could not have possibly known about when the order was written down.

I would like to divide the rest of the chapter into four areas of focus to consider when preparing an order of worship: time, tempo, transition, and trust. We will discuss them in what I feel is their order of importance.

Time

Take the time to listen to God. I told someone recently I have found God to be the great procrastinator in my life. He never speaks as quickly as I prefer; rather, He puts off telling me what He is up to until the last minute. Surely He knows how much I have to get done this week and how Sunday comes every seven days. How can He expect me to *be still and know* when there is so little time to begin with?

Have you ever noticed how much easier it is to hear God when you are already talking to Him? Be specific in your prayers. Pray for those on the platform *and* in the congregation. Lift the needs you know about and those that only God is aware of. We cannot do this on our own strength or in our own wisdom.

Years ago someone asked me if I was ever afraid that one day I would wake up and not be able to write another song. My response was that I really do not worry about that anymore.

Through the years I have learned enough about the craft of writing and how to use poetic devices that I would always be able to write a song. What scared me a whole lot more was the fact that I had learned enough about the craft to write a song from my own strength. That is the kind of song almost guaranteed to move no one, and it is not the kind of song I want my name on.

The same thing holds true when creating an order of worship. There are plenty of resources available in books, on the Internet, and in the church file drawer to give us more than enough options. The problem is that we may be missing out on what God wants to do in us and through us on any given Sunday. Without the time spent with God, we are only putting song titles on paper.

Tempo

I want to spend a little more time on tempo than on the others. Most elementary school students can tell you that tempo is the speed at which a song is performed, but that is not the tempo I am referring to here. Instead, I would like to spend a few minutes discussing the tempo or flow in the context of a worship service. In most churches the average time of the service devoted to worship is twenty minutes. Many variables can affect this, such as if you have a choir, if music is going on during the offering, and if you regularly include special music. As you begin to map out the tempo of the music section, the following questions become relevant:

- Does the congregation stand or sit during worship time?

- Are you blessed with live musicians or do you rely on soundtracks?
- Does the offering come in the middle of the music package?
- What about prayer? Do you lead the prayer or does the pastor?
- How does the pastor prefer the table to be set?

All of these are valid considerations, and hopefully you are breaking the patterns enough that none of these questions can be answered with a simple yes or no or the same answer every week. I have talked to some worship leaders who always start with an up-tempo song and always end with a prayer song. There is nothing wrong with that unless you use the same pattern every Sunday.

Have you ever been working in a room with the television on but you aren't watching it? What happens if a commercial comes on with no volume? If you are like most people, you instinctively look up at the set to see what's wrong. It's a great advertising technique because it relies on the fact that we grow accustomed to patterns or the *tempo* of noise. In similar fashion, if you start every Sunday up and end down, before long the tempo of the service will become familiar and the congregation will lose interest.

An old adage used by publishers when talking to writers and arrangers of church musicals is to start big and end bigger. For the most part, that formula is followed. One of my favorite all-time Christmas musicals is a 1988 project called "Noel" arranged by Don Marsh. He was paired with songwriter Lanny Wolfe and one of my heroes, the late Bob Benson, who wrote the narration. Anyone who has been around church music on any level realizes this is a pretty powerful trio. Yet what I remember years later is the intro to the opening song—a lone gut string guitar playing an eleven-note pattern. After repeating the pattern a few times, the orchestra took its place alongside the simple melody, and the musical was born. It was so different from everything else in the marketplace that it caught my attention and drew me into the project immediately.

There are other ways to establish the tempo of a worship service. Placing your songs in a fast, slow, fast, slow progression is as interesting as sitting boy, girl, boy, girl used to be as a kid. If variety becomes predictable, it can no longer be called variety. Do you normally talk between songs? Are your musical introductions consistently reduced to the last line of the chorus? If so, chances are good that everyone in the church can predict where you are going and how you are going to get there. Map out your moments and, whenever possible, select songs with lyrics that move in a deliberate sequence. For example, don't follow up a song about heaven with a song about the cross. They are both wonderful and valid song topics, yet they lead the congregation to two different destinations. I will be the first to admit most people will not notice things as subtle as this, but they can still sense when the order of worship feels right and when it doesn't.

One of the most important but often overlooked factors creating a good tempo for a worship package is the third T.

Transition

I cannot begin to tell you how many great moments are lost due to the lack of a good transition. If you give careful consideration to the key and time signature of a song, you can find built-in transitions. For example, if you choose four different songs with the first one in the key of C, the second song in the key of D, the third in the key of G and the fourth in the key of C, each transition has the appearance of lifting into the next song, only to end up where you started.

It's also wise to keep a running list of good transitions. If you notice two songs such as "How Great Is Our God" and "How Great Thou Art" go well together, write it down so you will remember it.

Depending on the level of your musicians, try going directly into the next song with only a transition chord to take them there. If a song is to be followed by the pastoral prayer, make sure the pastor knows at exactly what point to come to the platform. If someone is singing a special, start the intro to the soundtrack while he or she is coming to the platform rather than waiting till the microphone is in hand. I realize I am a little oversensitive at times, but attention to this will take the flow of your worship to a new level of communication effectiveness.

A good measure of tempo and transition is to listen to an audio recording of your service without a video. You might be surprised how much dead time you hear on the recording. Barring unforeseen circumstances, those dead spaces can be tightened up with very little effort.

One of the hardest transitions for many churches is to know what to do after playing a video. Because media—which will be discussed in a later chapter—is new to many churches, the end of the video is often followed by an awkward silence. The congregation doesn't know whether or not to applaud, and the effectiveness of the video is lessened in the process.

One suggestion is to analyze what is going on at the end of the video. Many commercial videos have some sort of a music bed playing in the background. Check which key it is in and have a song ready to start in the same key even as the video is fading to black. If there is no music, use the time when the lights are down to move the next speaker to the center of the platform ready to go the very instant the video ends. One of the goals of any worship leader is to lead the people into worship and help set the table for the pastor. Involve your pastor to be part of the dialog. If what you are doing is not working, try something else.

Trust

If you're like me, sometimes the hardest part of creating an order of worship is letting go with the confidence that it is right. Proverbs 3:5 (KJV) tells us to "Trust in the LORD with all thine heart; and lean not unto thine own understanding," but often that is easier said than done. After all, didn't they hire you to do this because of your understanding of what is involved? Let me ask you a question: Do you really think those instincts originated with you? What I am talking about is declaring your dependency on God to lead and then trusting where He takes you.

This seems like a good place to interject what I have learned about trust: There is a very direct correlation between my trust in God for today and His faithfulness in days past. If I really take the time to listen to God, and I trust what He is saying, He gives me peace in the process. I don't have to wrestle with, reexamine, or second-guess the order of worship. I have seen it over and over again through the years, and to paraphrase Isaiah 55:8, His ideas are always going to be way better than mine will ever be. I just need to learn to trust Him and quit depending on me.

We began this chapter by talking about the need for preparation. While it is true that Sunday comes every seven days, planning for worship happens on all seven days. Expose yourself to new music whenever possible. Even if you are bi-vocational, find the time to stay inspired. If you need a Sunday off, take a Sunday off. Burnout is as close as you allow it to be. The joys of leading worship are too many to miss—and they too come every seven days.

The Promise: "My God shall supply all your need according to his riches in glory by Christ Jesus" (Philippians 4:19, KJV).

The Prayer: *Lord, work in me and through me to point your children to you. Inhabit our praise, and give us a glimpse of your glory.*

Contemplation Questions

1. What are some of the advantages of preparing further in advance than what you do now? Disadvantages?

2. Are you passionate about the details of the order of worship, or do think of yourself as more of a big-picture thinker?

3. Do you try to maintain a familiar worship tempo from week to week, or do you intentionally mix it up each week?

4. Do you dialogue with others on staff about the importance of transitions, or is is totally up to you?

5. What does letting worship "breathe" mean to you?

6

Rate
of Refresh

You are suffering from burnout. You can call it other things if you prefer, but at the end of the day the tank is on empty, and the worst part of all is that you cannot tell anyone. After all, you are the worship leader. It is your calling and your job to be endlessly upbeat and enthusiastic with enough energy to inspire everyone you come in contact with.

To celebrate my recent birthday, my wife, Cindi, said she was going to buy me a new television set. We have been married enough years that she has learned that when it comes to anything electronic or gadget-related, I prefer to pick it out myself. Even though I pride myself on staying somewhat current in this information age, I found myself more than a little overwhelmed by all the options available. Because this new television set had to fit within the confines of an existing bedroom shelf unit, the size was predetermined. Still, there were a dozen price ranges, including some from the same manufacturer.

I quickly learned that the difference between these television sets was determined by something called the *refresh rate*. Although I could not tell the difference by looking at them, I obviously opted for the model with the higher refresh rate, because—well, just in case it mattered. Only after I got home and did some research did I understand what the big deal was. The long answer involves words like cathode ray tubes and dividing the horizontal scan rate by the number of horizontal pixels and multiplying the result by .95. The short answer simply means the number of times a screen is "re-painted" per second.

Although you may be able to feel stress coming, burnout can hit you before you see it coming. With stress, you want to try harder, while burnout causes you to want to do nothing at all.

Have you ever stopped to consider what your refresh rate is? An even more important question to ask yourself is *What am I doing to ensure I am staying refreshed?*

I would think most bi-vocational worship leaders are more than slightly amused when they hear the phrase "part-time minister of music." From what I have discovered, there is very little about the job that is part-time anything. You come home at the end of your regular workday to spend time on special music schedules, preview new music, plan offertories, prepare PowerPoint slides, and endlessly look ahead to the next musical. On Sunday you are often the first one there and the last to leave, and by default you become platform janitor, music librarian, and recruiter-in-chief for any and all things musical.

Is it any wonder the burnout rate is so high? Even those who have not reached the point of total despair might recognize some of the symptoms. I suspect we all have days when, no matter what we do, we feel no one notices or cares. The part of the job that once excited us the most is now an arduous process.

There is no shortage of books written by competent authors on overcoming burnout in the workplace, but this is not that book, and I am not that author. I wish I had a one-size-fits-all approach that would immediately pull us out of the funk when it finds us. But since I don't, I think we would be better served to back up and talk about some ways to avoid it at the outset. As you've probably already discovered, my approach to anything is to try and reduce it to the basics. Thomas Edison once said, "Always make it as simple as possible, but never simpler," and that is the approach I intend to take with this topic as well.

Looking back at my own encounters with burnout, they share two common attributes, with one being the cause and the other the cure. In the cause column, stress is almost always at or near the top of my list; and for me the quickest road back usually begins with something as simple as encouragement.

I realize the word *stress* is pretty nonspecific and can be affixed to a whole myriad of situations; however, stress is not the same thing as burnout. Although it can be one of the roads that *leads* to burnout, the two are fundamentally different. Stress is caused from too many demands, while burnout is about a well that is dried up. Although you may be able to feel stress coming, burnout can hit you before you see it coming. With stress, you want to try harder, while burnout causes you to want to do nothing at all.

For me personally, stress is usually brought on by the fact that I have committed to too many things to too many people. As Henry Kissinger said, "There cannot be a stressful crisis next week. My schedule is already full." I remember all too well the abuse I took from my friends when I stayed up all night finishing a school paper on the importance of time management. I know it sounds funny, but unfortunately it is an all-too-accurate synopsis of where I find myself more often than I wish.

I spoke in an earlier chapter about how the church can take as much as we will give, and I believe that to be the case. Added to that is the pressure we often feel to lead by example.

The problem is that often those we are trying to lead are content to let us do it all. To make matters worse, most of us have found at a certain point that it is easier to do it ourselves so we know it will be done the way we want it.

One of the best pieces of advice I received concerning the dangers of an overcrowded schedule came from my pastor, who challenged me to make a list of everything I do during the course of a normal week. He said to then look at what things on that list could be done by someone other than me. It sounds easy enough, but it proved to be much harder than I imagined. Sure, someone else could set out the music for choir practice or straighten the chairs, but how about doing the choir newsletter or entering the songs in the computer? After all, I like things to be done in a certain way.

The truth is, there is almost always more than one right answer, and just because it may not be the way I would have done it does not make it wrong. I know one of the toughest parts of leadership is learning to let go, but one of the greatest attributes of leadership is the ability to do so.

Maybe you have a Brenda in your church. Brenda was a great organizer. In fact, Brenda was good at a whole lot of things. As a singer, she could carry a solo as well as anyone else in the church. Her rich alto voice combined with the ability to read music made her the ideal choir member. She was a prayer warrior and a team player. She had my back when it needed protecting and wasn't afraid to ask questions when they needed asking.

But here's the problem. It turns out that Brenda stressed easily, and the list of things she stressed over was the complete opposite of my list. She worried about whether or not the chairs in the choir room were in the same formation as they were in the choir loft on the platform. She was also concerned with the choir lining up in the right order before they walked onto the platform and if there was a specific dress code for the upcoming musical. Not that those things weren't important—they just weren't important to me. Asking Brenda to be in charge of all those things helped ease both her stress level and mine.

We talked in an earlier chapter about investment strategies. Another form of investment comes when we not only allow but also encourage people to use the gifts God has given them. If you're wishing you had people like Brenda so you could empower them, I ask you—when was the last time you allowed yourself to be vulnerable enough with your people to let them know you needed help? A misconception among many leaders is that they always have to know all the answers, anticipate every situation, and "never let them see you sweat" in the process. More often than not, there are people sitting in the church waiting to be asked to serve in places you haven't even identified as needs yet.

One more thing I would add when it comes to avoiding burnout is to learn to include rest in your schedule. For some of us, this is a challenge. I know all the tricks and can even attempt to justify the busy pace, because I genuinely enjoy what I do. I have even been known to plan things on my day off without writing it on the calendar, as if this somehow makes it less official.

Years ago I served on a church board that was interviewing prospective new pastors. One by one we went through the list of names under consideration. I remember being amazed as I watched one of the candidates all but eliminated because his résumé showed he had taken a sabbatical. The presumption was that there must have been a problem with his ministry that he needed to escape. I responded that even though I did not know this particular pastor, I think churches in general would be in better shape if every staff member were required to take a sabbatical. I sometimes wonder if the greatest realization about taking a needed rest may also be the greatest fear. And that is to discover that the world can keep on spinning and the church can keep on being the church even if we are not there.

If stress sounds like an over-simplistic cause, then encouragement can likewise be viewed as the cure. I am not sure when things changed in the life of the Church, but somewhere along the way, music—and therefore the minister of music—became a lightning rod for complaints and complainers. With all the hours a worship leader puts in and the amount of heart equity invested in the music program, it is amazing how much his or her state of mind can be positively affected by a little encouragement.

I have heard it said about the person running audio that if he or she is doing the job well, no one notices there is someone even there. Unfortunately, that seems to have spilled over to the worship leader as well. In many churches, people are quick to vocalize their complaints yet slow to offer encouragement. At the end of the day, we all desire and need to know that someone notices our efforts. Many people talk about how we have only to please an audience of one. And even though we know that to be true in our hearts, the human in us needs to be confirmed in a way we can get our hands around.

So how do we accomplish something so basic? It may sound strange, but it takes courage to be an encourager. Yet by doing so, we have a great opportunity to lead by example. What do you think would happen if you showed up for choir practice or a music committee meeting with a box of stationery and a roll of stamps, shared a devotional from Luke 17 about the Samaritan who was healed and returned to thank Jesus, and then challenged each person present to write a thank-you note to someone?

When I traveled in a weekend ministry, I felt that the ministry God had for me was not a pulpit ministry but rather to encourage discouraged music ministers. It seemed that everywhere I went I encountered weary and frustrated servants who just needed to know they were not alone. Thus, when I felt God calling me to a church, I feared that I, too, might become like that. Armed more out of fear than wisdom, I set out to put some safeguards in place hopefully to avoid these pitfalls. First I decided that I would find sources of encouragement that were not directly dependent on what people did or said. Instead, I looked for other measures such as watching the light come on in someone's eyes as the song became personal, or seeing the attendance grow in choir practice.

Of all the things I tried, one in particular had the longest-reaching effect. From my very first day I decided to keep every thank-you note I received in one of my desk drawers.

Some of them were simple notes from people telling me they were praying for me. Others were specific notes of encouragement for a musical or special event. My thinking was that on the days I was feeling most discouraged I would go to the drawer and read them. Here is the great part of the story: When I resigned after four and a half years at that church, while cleaning out my desk, I realized I had never felt the need to open the drawer one single time. I owe it to the fact that not only was I blessed to lead some truly amazing people, but I also had learned to find encouragement in places most people would not have looked.

The Promise: "The LORD himself goes before you and will be with you; he will never leave you nor forsake you. Do not be afraid; do not be discouraged" (Deuteronomy 31:8, NIV).

The Prayer: *Lord, remind me that I am about your work. Surround me with reminders that not only have you called me, but you will also be faithful to complete your work in and through me.*

Contemplation Questions

1. Are you aware when burnout is approaching, or do you not see it coming until it hits you?

2. When life outside the church becomes stressful, does your heart run toward or away from ministry?

3. Do you seek out encouragers when you need them, or do they find you?

4. What are you doing that someone else could do as well as or better than you?

5. Did you buy this book for yourself, or did someone buy it for you?

7

A Picture Is Worth a Thousand Distractions

Up until now you've avoided the whole issue of projector screens in the sanctuary, but the moment of reckoning has finally come. You're not even sure where to begin the process at this point. Even if you can make the transition, it sounds like a whole new layer of things you will have to oversee that have the possibility of going wrong. Is it really worth it?

One of the greatest surprises for many ministers of music is the ever-changing job description. Even those who have held the position for long periods of time find themselves faced with weekly responsibilities that were never mentioned in the interview yet now fall under their direction. One that can be the most intimidating is the ministry of media. I call it a ministry, because when done well, it can have as much positive impact on the service as the ministry on the platform. But like many other topics discussed in this book, the opposite also holds true. When media is not done well, it can absolutely destroy the flow of what is going on. Therein lies part of the problem for the church finding itself standing on the water's edge, afraid to get its toes wet. There is far too much at stake financially—as well as potential impact on the service—to do it halfway.

Though music is only one of the four main media food groups (music, videos, announcements, and sermon aids), in almost every situation I have seen, the responsibility for this ministry defaults to the minister of music. To complicate matters even further, in most cases in which media is used, it is operated by someone other than the music minister and viewed by everyone in the church except the music minister

Though music is only one of the four main media food groups (music, videos, announcements, and sermon aids), in almost every situation I have seen, the responsibility for this ministry defaults to the minister of music.

because the screen is behind his or her back, unless there is also a projector aimed at the back of the sanctuary.

I was tempted to call this chapter "If You Don't Do Media, Then Don't Do Media," because I firmly believe that unless you have an understanding of all the technological peculiarities associated with this ministry, you may want to consider waiting until you find someone who does. The learning curve is high, and so are the potential frustrations you will undoubtedly face. If I have not scared you off yet, it is probably safe to continue reading.

The remainder of this chapter will be written with the assumption that even though you are not the person operating the media equipment, you will be the one who in large part defines the thinking behind it. My personal views began to come into focus several years ago when I was visiting a large church just north of Cincinnati, Ohio, pastored by my good friend David Graves. As he showed me the recently purchased, state-of-the-art, expensive sound system, I asked him if it was a tough sell to convince the congregation to spend the money.

I will never forget his response to me: "It really was not. We are in the business of communication, and we need to communicate at the highest level possible."

Even though the focus of this chapter is media, I trust you will read it within the bigger context stated by Pastor Graves, which *is* communication.

Because the field of technology is changing by the week, it would serve little purpose in a book of this nature to include specific equipment recommendations. However, if you are presently serving at a church that does not use media, or you are contemplating an equipment upgrade, following are some simple basics to consider in your selection process. Some of this media information will overlap with the chapter on audio, especially in regard to budget. As strongly as I can state it, try to avoid the mistake that many small—and some large— churches make of letting price alone determine the purchases.

I would also add the importance of parallel priorities when it comes to your shopping list. For example, don't buy the best screen available only to cut corners on the projector. This is like buying a new Mercedes and putting a go-cart engine in it. It would look great but wouldn't even begin to accomplish its intended purpose. Spend your money wisely and evenly, or hold off on spending altogether. If you have not previously used media, you are probably going out on a limb to convince your people of its potential positive impact. Don't destroy that trust, or you may not get it back again.

After considering what you desire to achieve by adding visual media, it is important to evaluate the basic factors of the presentation system.

Sources

What are you displaying? DVD, Powerpoint/Easy Worship, Camera Image Magnification?

System Switching, Processing, and Distribution

System switching, processing, and distribution is easily the most overlooked area of the video system, but it is the most important, as you need to determine how you get the sources listed above to the screen or screens. Each of these may be a different video format, and all may need to be used on the screens in a given service. For this reason you must answer the following questions:

- How will my sources get to the projector to be displayed?
- Will I run separate signals from each component to the projector and use its infrared remote to switch between the devices? While this works, it can become a big area of distraction due to the fact that every time you switch inputs on the projector, it tells you that on the screen.
- Am I using multiple projectors? In that scenario you also have to include distribution amplifiers for each of the sources.
- Should I utilize a scaling switcher to control my sources at the control location?

These are questions that can be evaluated only by your individual needs. I mention them here, however, so that they are not overlooked.

Projector

With the many models on the market today, selecting projectors can be challenging. Here are the basic things to consider:

- *What size and type screen will I be using?* This will determine how bright your projector will need to be.
- *Where will my projector be mounted?* Besides the size of the screen, this must be considered in order to assure you have adequate throw distance to fill the screen.

- *What aspect ratio will I be using?* Today more than ever you must decide if you are primarily planning to utilize 16:9 or 4:3 aspect ratios.

- *What resolution do I need?* As with computer monitors, all projectors have a native resolution (1024x768, 1280x720 and so on). This resolution will determine the cost of the projector itself. High resolution in large-screen projection isn't always necessary, however, particularly in the church setting. In fact, unless you are looking close-up at fine CAD drawings or tiny numbers on a spreadsheet, the overall resolution is wasted on large fonts and .jpg graphics.

- *What is the overall contrast ratio?* This rating is as important as the ANSI lumen rating of the projector. The ability to make dark blacks directly affects the perception of white brightness in a projection or display system.

Projector Mount

The projector mount is easily overlooked, but it is necessary to the system. Most projectors must be centered either at the top or bottom edge of the projection screen. Mounting above or below, left or right of center, will cause a keystone effect. Many modern projectors have lens shift options that can correct some errors in projector placement, but this is not usually found on inexpensive models. Most models also offer some type of electronic keystone correction. However, I don't recommend using this unless absolutely necessary, as it reduces overall resolution and often leaves undesired artifacts to the image. Simply put, nothing can substitute for an optimally placed projector. Whether it is floor mounted, ceiling mounted, front or rear projection, these basic principles apply.

Screens—Size, Placement, and Surface

Screen systems can be diverse and expensive; they can also make or break your video system. First, consider *placement.* To be effective, the screen or screens should be placed on axis view of the platform and be easily viewable by the entire congregation. If the congregation's view must be removed from the platform in order to view the screens, the effectiveness of your media may be compromised. The media should be considered as a supporting part of the worship service, and it is difficult to maintain this effect if the viewer must continually look away from the platform in order to watch the media.

Screen size. Bigger is not always better. Screens should be big enough for the entire audience to clearly see the images projected; however, screens that overwhelm the architecture or the look of a given space can be distracting. Keep this in mind when selecting the screen size.

Placement. As mentioned above, it is important to consider the throw distance of your projector to ensure you have adequate distance to fully fill the screen surface. The screen should be placed in an area where you can control the amount of ambient light spill on the screen surface, as ambient light is the biggest natural enemy of top-quality projection.

Screen surfaces. Many believe that a light-colored wall is adequate as a projection surface. While this can be done, it seldom produces accurate color reproduction, nor is it as effective as a screen surface or screen paints such as Screen Goo. The main advantage of screens—particularly tensioned screens—is to provide an accurately sized, shaped, flat, even surface on which to project. Paints and wall surfaces, even under the best of situations, have surface imperfections that are detrimental to the image. Many screen surfaces purchased from companies such as Da-Lite or Stewart will have gain ratings and/or high-contrast options. These refer to the reflectiveness of the screen surface. High-gain screens will reflect more light back to the viewer but often sacrifice the viewing angle to achieve this effect, that is, the image grows dimmer as you move off to the sides of the screen. Lower-gain screens usually have wider viewing angles. High-contrast screens can be effective in certain situations but may have a negative effect in situations with direct ambient light on the screens.

Slides

For those of you who already have a projector and screen in place, let's talk for a minute about lyric slide philosophy. When visitors come to your church, the last thing you want is for their first impression to be a distraction. Hard-to-read slides or lyrics that are either different from what is being sung or in the wrong sequence can be deadly to the flow of worship. How do you prevent this from happening? If you figure out a way to totally eliminate the problem, let me know. Until then, let me suggest a few fundamental things to help lead you toward a worship experience that is as distraction-free as possible.

While most of us would agree the technological ability required to advance a slide to the next screen is so minimal that almost anyone can do it, the opposite is true. In far too many cases, that is also the first symptom of the eventual problem. We approach it as if getting to the next slide is all that matters. I have known more than a few ministers of music who ask their musicians to show up early enough to rehearse, yet do not ask the same of the media operator. I cannot overstate the importance of everyone being there at the same time and on the same page. It is not enough to simply turn in your order of worship to whoever is doing the media and expect it to be right. In fact, I can almost guarantee it will not be. Just like everything else, getting it right requires practice. It also requires equal investment, spiritual focus, rehearsal time, and respect. Far be it from me to suggest that a media operator might intentionally sabotage a service—but just to be on the safe side, treat him or her well. I do not need to remind you that the media operator can make you look either very good or very bad.

Keith Sealy is a long-time friend who oversees the media at my church. He does it as professionally as I have ever seen it done, and through the years he has developed some strong opinions and solid instincts. He points out that the training of volunteers is a big part of having a successful media team. In his words: "You cannot just put someone at the video station and expect them to know what to do. They have to know what each piece of equipment does and how to use that piece of equipment."

I would add that if you are blessed to have someone capable of running your media *and* willing to mentor others, take advantage of it. Also make sure you add your own name to the list of students. Even though you will not be the operator, at some point you are sure to be asked questions about the process—because, after all, you are the minister of music. Learn what you can when you can from whomever you can—even if you are convinced you will never need to use it.

Slide Appearance

A theory often referred to as the 5X5 rule states that you should never have more than five lines on one slide or more than five words in a line. Like any other rule, there are times this can be broken without anyone getting hurt, but it is a good one to keep in mind.

While more and more software presentation applications include some form of access to lyrics, eventually you will want to do a song that is not found in your database. In a perfect world, I would have whoever is going to be operating the projector on Sunday be the same one who enters the text into the slides. There are several reasons this is preferable, but mainly it's so the operator has a chance to live with the lyrics long before Sunday. Let him or her listen to an audio copy of the song so he or she can pace how the lyrics appear on the screen to how it will be sung. One of the most frustrating and distracting things is to stand in the congregation when the music minister is trying to teach a new song for the first time and the lines on the screen do not break the same place as the music. If you are the one doing the leading, you may not even be aware of the reason the congregation seems so slow to catch on to what you are sure is a good song.

I have also heard those who claim to know say you should never stay on one screen for more than seven seconds. I assume this has something to do with people like me with short attention spans whose minds begin to wander after that amount of time.

Fonts

There are also some basic rules of thumb when it comes to fonts, font sizes, and word counts that are worth mentioning here. If you go to all the trouble to type lyrics onto a slide, it makes sense for the congregation to be able to read them. I personally prefer a "bolder is better" approach. If you are unsure of which font to use, Arial is a good place to start. It is non-distracting and very easy to read.

When it comes to font size, one suggestion is to take the age of the oldest person in the room, divide that number by half, and you have your ideal font size. Many of you have at least one or two seasoned citizens attending your church who would throw that formula a little out of line, but it is something to consider. A safer approach may be to use a font size near forty for lyrics (never below thirty) and somewhere between forty-six and sixty for the song title. You should almost never change fonts within a song, however.

Presentation 101 tells us that contrast is a good thing when choosing font color and how it relates to the background texture. In addition to the font color, making good use of drop shadows or outlining the text can also add life to the screen.

Some churches new to media take the concepts of simplicity and contrast too far and are content to put white type on a black screen. Unless you are printing a handout, this combination of colors is almost guaranteed to suck the life out of any great song.

Special Effects

As long as I am listing my personal pet peeves, I should not leave out the person who attempts to use every transition or text animation available to him or her in every song. One of the characteristics that sets apart the beginner from the experienced is knowing how *little* to use special effects. Remember: the goal is communicating what you want them to know in a way that is not distracting. Just because the software will do something cool does not mean you should feel compelled to use it. When it comes to bells and whistles, less is almost always more. Starting out simple also means avoiding overuse of graphics. Find a nice background image—most applications offer free options—and stick with it. The main goal is to focus on the lyrics, not the background.

Always Have a Plan B

No matter how hard you work and prepare, you must be prepared to deal with what I call "Murphy's Law of Worship." That is, "Anything that can go wrong will go wrong and always happens on Sunday morning." A few months ago I was in Atlanta making a presentation to a roomful of ministers of music. I had checked the DVD several times, and it worked perfectly. As you can guess, when it came time to play it, the DVD player decided to shut down. Imagine my surprise when everyone in the room started laughing and applauding. It dawned on me that they all had been there and knew exactly how it felt.

I have heard it said that a good baseball player decides before every pitch what he is going to do with the ball if it comes to him. In the same manner, you will save yourself a lot of trouble by coming to grips with the fact that equipment will malfunction. It is not a matter of *if,* but *when.* Always have a backup plan that allows you to anticipate rather than react. Decide in advance what you are going to do at any given moment should Murphy's Law of Worship make an unexpected visit to your service.

I want to close this chapter where it began. We are in the communication business. Every element that is added is one more place for potential breakdown. If you are like me, you remember a great visual more often than what you heard spoken or sung. As you look for new and fresh ways to tell the story, media opens up a whole world of opportunity to make a difference in the life of your church. Because of its potential impact, it deserves the very best we can give it.

The Promise : "If any of you lacks wisdom, he should ask God, who gives generously to all without finding fault, and it will be given to him" (James 1:5).

The Prayer: *Lord, I pray that you cover us with your wisdom as we seek to tell your story to those you bring us in contact with.*

Contemplation Questions

1. Did you inherit the responsibility of media, or did you take it out of frustration with how it used to be?

2. Do you think of your media operator as part of your ministry team?

3. When you have the chance to visit other churches or special events, do you try to figure out what font they are using?

4. Have you been able to effectively translate your passion for a media ministry?

5. Did you help choose the colors in your own home? (that is, do you trust your eye when it comes to color?).

8

Do You Hear What I Hear?

How hard can it be? I mean, after all, common sense says that if someone is walking to the center of the platform and picking up a microphone, he or she has every intention of speaking into it. Is it just my church that struggles with this issue?

Periodically throughout this book I have made reference to the small church in Michigan I attended growing up. It was a part of who I was then and in large measure helped shape who I am today. When I look back on those days, one of the memories that still causes me to laugh concerns one of its earlier audio systems.

I'm not saying that the small Shure microphone mixer with six knobs plus an on-off switch was not sufficient for our needs. But what intrigued me even as a young boy was where they chose to install it. You had to know where it was to see it. In fact, if my father had not been in the choir, it may have remained a mystery. In the choir room, behind the racks of choir robes, inside a wooden cabinet complete with lock, was audio grand central for our sanctuary. After all these years, I am undecided whether the lock was to deter theft or keep people from adjusting the volume. The one thing I knew for certain was that the minister of music held the key.

In that respect, not too much has really changed. Even today with all the technological advancements in audio, I still maintain that the minister of music should hold the key to the overall approach to audio in the church. While I'm quite certain all my friends who do audio professionally would disagree with my assumptions, my proverbial heels are pretty dug in on the topic.

Let me explain how I arrived at this conclusion. It does not matter if the sound is too loud, if there is a low frequency hum in the system, or the soundtrack overwhelms the voices. Inevitably the complaints will eventually land on your desk. (I have a theory on that, too, but I'll save that for a later book.) As you have already discovered, ministers of music are often judged just as much by what they can control as what they cannot. It is extremely frustrating and discouraging to diligently work on song selection and flow of service during the week only to have its impact diminished by an audio operator who is on a different page.

Frank Luntz is a political pollster and frequent guest on one of the cable news shows. His specialty is gauging people's reactions to political speeches. He puts focus groups in a room, and through a complex series of graphs, he is supposedly able to show what the listener reacts to most passionately and when opinions are changed. Whenever I watch him, I find myself wondering what it would be like to use his system on a typical Sunday morning congregation to gauge how people relate to audio. I suspect we might all be surprised at the influence good non-distracting audio plays in how we communicate worship.

Years ago when I traveled in solo ministry, I built a little gadget that intrigued many music ministers. It was a little black wooden box with three buttons by which I could control the cassette deck and audio with my foot. One button started the tape, the middle button stopped it, and the third button was a reverb bypass switch. I am quick to admit that I am not an electrician, and it took many attempts to get it working just as I wanted, but eventually I could seamlessly control the pace of the service without depending on the timing of someone I didn't know. Through the years I lost count of the music ministers who asked if there was something like it available commercially. I knew what they wanted was not my little foot pedal system as much as the control it offered.

When I say the minister of music should hold the key to audio, I am not talking about taking it to that extreme, nor am I suggesting you become a micromanager of fader positions or even microphone placement. What I am referring to is having a voice in defining your church's audio philosophy. You may be one of the truly blessed who has the perfect audio person at your church. If so, do yourself and your church a huge favor by listening to his or her input. The dialog will be invaluable from a mutual trust standpoint as chances are good that you will learn from each other.

How do I define the perfect audio person? For me, it involves three characteristics—an ear for music, a mind for electronics, and a heart for God. I am very aware, however, that many churches have to settle for one or maybe two of these attributes. If that is your situation, it is also your re-sponsibility to help this person continue to grow in the areas in which he or she is weak. Talk about what was and was not effective in the service, and discuss possible ways to make it better. It also helps to keep your philosophy in front of the person. (For those of you who are interested, I also have a definition of a worst-case scenario in which you have some-one running audio who does not have even one of the three perfect-scenario characteristics listed above yet is under the impression that he or she possess all three.)

What is your audio philosophy? Have you thought about it enough to actually write it out on paper? And are your priorities the same as the person running the sound at your church? Having that person write out his or her list and compare it with yours could help explain why some things are not working. Let me give you an example. If I were writing out my list of priorities for the person running audio, it might read something like the following.

1. Prepare

Do not wait until Sunday morning to prepare for the worship service. Ask questions ahead of time. Will there be any solos in the service? Will the choir or special music be using a soundtrack? Is there a special offertory? How many microphones will be used during the service?

While these may seem like basic and obvious questions, waiting until Sunday morning to ask them only increases the chances of something unexpected going wrong. (See Murphy's Law of Worship in chapter 7.) The goal is to remove as much stress from the process as possible. If you know ahead of time that there will be more involved than normal, you can adjust your schedule accordingly.

One of the easiest areas for improvement is to remove extra microphones from the platform. It might surprise you how much can be accomplished by doing something so simple. For one thing, it just looks better. I have been in some churches where there was enough excess microphone cable lying on the floor of the platform that the singers could have sung from the parking lot.

My pastor recently challenged each staff member to walk through his or her area of ministry and try to look at it through a visitor's eyes. I have to admit that when I did this, the platform looked a whole lot more cluttered than I realized. I found music from weeks before stacked on the edge of the piano and even an empty water bottle by a choir chair. A similar walkthrough might surprise you.

Another reason to clear the platform of unused audio equipment is the possibility a soloist might pick up a different microphone than what the audio operator is expecting. Anything that holds even the slightest potential of breaking the flow of the service should be eliminated whenever possible. Even if the microphones are color coded in one form or another, it can raise the heart rate of both the soloist and the audio operator while they try to get the right fader pulled up.

2. Anticipation

Most of you probably laughed when you read the chapter opener. For others of you, it may have hit a little too close to home to be funny. When it comes to the microphone not being turned up in time, this is not an issue that happens just in small churches. In fact, you may have heard one or more variations on the old joke that says, "Show me a microphone, and I'll show you an audio operator who will forget to turn it on." We have all seen it and experienced the frustration it causes. The problem is that eventually it becomes like the Mark Twain quote—"Everybody talks about the weather, but nobody does anything about it."

Some of you reading this may be convinced that there *is* nothing that can be done about it. While I agree that you cannot personally go back and turn the fader up, there are some things you can do to lower the risk. Do you actually follow the order of worship as it is printed, or are you prone to spontaneous changes? Also, is the microphone that will be used in the same place when it is not being used? I have seen situations in which someone using a handheld mic takes it down and sits on the front row, gets up, and starts talking as she makes her way to the platform and then wonders why the fader is not turned up.

I also want to suggest something for those of you who live in an imperfect world: If this is an ongoing problem, you might get in the habit of picking up the microphone but waiting two seconds before you say anything. This may not be ideal, but it is preferable to losing the first words or notes.

3. Maintenance

First, let me state something you already know for sure: equipment will eventually break down. Microphones, cables, power amps, consoles, and CD players—plus anything else you use—will go bad at some point. Even if any of the items listed above have only an intermittent problem, they are already useless. What you may also know but occasionally lose sight of is the level of distraction caused by equipment either going bad or already broken.

This is one reason the need for maintenance is high on my list of audio priorities. Everyone knows when buying a car that the price listed on the bill of sale is only the initial investment. Oil has to be changed, tires replaced, and on and on. It is no different when purchasing audio equipment. I would suspect many of you have found yourselves in the uncomfortable position of convincing your church to spend money on new equipment only to have to go back and ask for more money to repair or replace pieces of it. If you have any say or sway when it comes to audio budgets, make sure the need for maintenance is accounted for up front. Many churches tend to lump audio and music into the same budget, forcing the minister of music to choose between new music and functional equipment. Someone in your church may be able to fix what's broken, but depending on what it is, it may be cheaper to replace it, especially when it comes to microphone cables.

As I stated earlier in this chapter, it is important to develop, define, and continue to refine your audio philosophy and along the way to invest others in your way of thinking. Even though you may drive the dialog, eventually everyone who comes through the doors will be affected by it, either for good or bad.

✳ ✳ ✳

Because this is intended to be a back-to-the-basics chapter on audio, it would be incomplete if I did not at least touch on one of the more common distractions with church audio. I am also going to give you an absolute fix for it. Are you ready? If you encounter feedback—TURN IT DOWN! Okay, seriously, that is about the extent of what I understand from the technological side of things. So rather than avoid this chapter altogether—and also in my effort to be fair and balanced—I met with a couple of good friends who do audio for a living: Eric Cornell of Cornell Media Group and Keith Sealy, who I mentioned in an earlier chapter. I asked them how they would approach this chapter. Not only are they both extremely knowledgeable about all things related to audio, but each has spent a great deal of time dealing directly with church audio as well. It was a fascinating dialog during which I asked questions on behalf of ministers of music, and they responded on behalf of audio operators everywhere. As you develop your audio philosophy, you would do well to include some of their insights.

One of the points the two men emphasized was to remind me that the audio can be only as good as what the operator is given to work with. If financial constraints limit the quality of equipment, it stands to reason the audio person cannot work miracles. This is not only the case with major pieces of equipment but also what people bring in of their own. For example, you may have a guitar player who brings in a cheap guitar with bad strings and plays through a bad amplifier.

The same principle applies to keyboards and soundtracks. Is there one among us who hasn't been handed a cassette track purchased in the seventies because Aunt Martha always liked that song? I personally am in favor of a CD-only policy. If it is not available in CD, the singer should probably consider looking for a newer song.

One advantage a larger church has is that there is usually more happening on the platform. If the guitar player and/or his instrument fail to measure up, the audio person can hide it a little easier. This is not an option in a small church. Remember—anything that sounds bad to begin with is only going to sound worse coming through big speakers.

Addressing the issue of what instruments actually need a microphone, Eric and Keith talked about it being more a matter of trying to control everything as much as possible. For example, if you mic a piano and it is too loud, you can turn it down or even turn it completely off. On the other hand, if there is no mic on the piano and you need to hear more of it, you're stuck. When there is no microphone, other than raising or lowering the lid, you are at the mercy of how hard your piano player plays. They both felt strongly about eliminating as much stage volume as possible. Because the person operating the audio cannot control volume on things like electric guitar amplifiers, this can totally defeat everything else happening, and there is nothing anyone can do about it.

This led to the inevitable discussion about drum sets and those who play them. Almost every audio person I have ever talked to prefers an electronic drum set as opposed to an acoustic one. Again, it comes to an issue of control. While I agree with the need for control, I am not personally a big fan of electronic drums. Since I am not a drummer, however, I would probably defer to the one actually playing them. I re-

Depending on the style of the song, the average age of the congregation, the sequence of the service, or in some cases, even the denomination of the church, what is appropriate may vary.

member a conversation I had with our church drummer when I first started at the church. I never once asked him to play quieter. In fact, I told him I wanted him to be aggressive and play like a leader and that it would be up to me to figure out a way to control the volume. The look in his eyes was priceless; I feel quite certain he had not been told that before. The result was that he became a better player in the process, and I learned some things about Plexiglas.

I mentioned earlier the importance of continuing to refine your audio philosophy. I experienced a shift in my own thinking when talking to Eric and Keith about something I have believed for a long time. After many years of traveling in ministry, I have steadfastly maintained that audio at many churches, especially smaller ones, was being hurt by ownership issues. I have been aware of several cases in which the person who bought the system got to run it regardless of his or her lack of qualifications to do so. I have also known of instances in which people who knew how to solder a microphone cable anointed themselves in charge, even if they had no ear for music whatsoever. Over time, it became easier for me to carry a portable system with me than to invade someone's space.

In our discussion, Eric and Keith brought out something I had not thought of before. It is very possible that rather than the audio person just being inflexible, the problem may be due to insecurity. Perhaps someone came in and set it up right, and the audio person is afraid that if he or she changes it, it may not get back to its original setting. Another point my friends stressed was the importance of being able to adjust and readjust in a short amount of time. This is difficult to do if you have too many people in the booth.

While I still maintain the importance of some kind of rotation system, after our conversation I see some things a little differently than before. For example, what do you do if there is no one available to be added to the rotation? First of all, I suggest you stop considering adults as your only option. With the ease and access kids have these days to computers, find teachable personalities and let them learn beside you. Start with something easy, such as hitting "start" and "stop" on the soundtrack. It may surprise you how much they can contribute.

Another point worth making in regard to your audio philosophy is that as important as it is to have one, sometimes volunteer personnel can make you wonder why you even bother. When that happens, just keep reminding yourself that the destination is worth the journey, and hang on for the ride. I recently heard about one pastor who had an audio operator who could never seem to find the right fader at the right time. The pastor decided the best solution was to replace all the microphones with ones that had on-off switches and turn all of them off. While that may be the complete opposite of what is right for most churches, and admittedly is not this pastor's first choice, it is the right philosophy for where his church is now. Sometimes the best plan is to be flexible.

One of the other topics I discussed with Eric and Keith was proper sanctuary volume. When I brought up the question, I fully expected the stock answer of between sixty and eight dB. What I got was something much more practical. Eric used a phrase I had not heard before: *appropriateness of level.*

(I wanted to ask whose version of appropriate, but I think I can guess what his response would have been.)

His point was that there are as many different variables as there are sanctuary styles and sizes. Depending on the style of the song, the average age of the congregation, the sequence of the service, or in some cases even the denomination of the church, what is appropriate may vary. If you are in a sanctuary with a large pipe organ, the appropriate level may differ significantly from the sanctuary with only a piano for instrumentation. When the choir is doing a special song, it is not uncommon for the audio operator to ride the gain as the song itself begins to swell. A good audio engineer can accomplish these variances without the congregation ever knowing anything happened.

While this chapter could conceivably go on indefinitely, I want to zero in on three final pieces of advice I feel are important.

First of all, people will always have opinions—mostly negative—about audio. If audio operators seem more than a little resistant to suggestions, it may very well be because they have had to endure an endless stream of complaints. I doubt many people make it a point to compliment them on a job well done. Therefore, the only comments they hear are negative. A minister of music can go a long way in the mentoring process by becoming the number-one encourager, thereby setting the example for the rest of the church.

I would also recommend implementing a policy that only you—or possibly the senior pastor—have the authority to state what is and what is not appropriate audio. I don't make this suggestion so you can constantly voice your opinion on the matter, but rather to give the audio operator an out when people complain or make requests. Yes, it means you are likely to hear a few more of the complaints, but by and large I believe people will be more respectful of your position and hopefully more considerate in their approaches than they would to the person running audio. You also are likely to win a friend for life in the person pushing the faders.

Last, if you are like me and have an audio philosophy but very little personal experience at an audio console, I suggest you not let that hold back your audio ministry. One of the best things you can do for your church is to arrange with a larger church in your area to allow your audio operator to go and observe for a few Sundays. Find a time that they can talk philosophy beforehand and then watch it come together on Sunday. The couple of weeks your operator will be gone can turn out to be one of the best investments you can make for the long term of your church audio.

The Promise: "May our Lord Jesus Christ himself and God our Father, who loved us and by his grace gave us eternal encouragement and good hope, encourage your hearts and strengthen you in every good deed and word" (2 Thessalonians 2:16).

The Prayer: *Lord, I pray that you encourage those today who are called to communicate your story. Show us your power at work within us.*

Contemplation Questions

1. Do you allow any one age group to sway your sound philosophy?

2. If there are consistent problems with the person running audio, do you try to be a mentor, or do you look for a replacement?

3. Can the congregation tell if you are frustrated?

4. Do you fight for budget for needed audio equipment with the same passion you fight for new music budget?

5. Do you evaluate your audio on a regular basis or only when something breaks?

9

Small-Choir
Rehearsal
Techniques

By Ed Hogan

About a year ago, before I had any idea I would be working on this book, I was in South Carolina on a business trip. That evening I went to dinner with some friends and was seated next to a man named Ed Hogan, whom I had not met before. The more he talked, the more I could sense his passion for the small church. Because his reputation as an arranger and clinician had preceded him, I began asking questions, and I was completely intrigued with his approach when it came to small-choir rehearsal techniques and small-church bands. When the call came to work on this book, I contacted him and asked if he would be willing to share his insights. As you read the next two chapters, I am certain you will be glad I asked him.

The Day of Small Things

Zechariah 4 is part of a fascinating story. God is raising up Zerubbabel to lead a remnant of Jews back to the decimated city of Jerusalem after seventy years of exile in Babylon. The most famous passage in the chapter is found in Zechariah 4:6, "This is the word of the LORD to Zerubbabel: 'Not by might nor by power, but by my Spirit,' says the LORD Almighty."

But the verse every small-choir director should look at carefully is verse 10, in which the prophet speaks to an overwhelmed leader and says, "Who despises the day of small things?" Have you ever felt that way? How about the Wednesday night rehearsal when only six people show up? Or the Sunday morning when only one alto sings? On those days, do you ever wish you were directing the big choir down the road?

Our encouragement lies in two important spiritual truths. First, God is sovereign over the circumstances of your life. He is in control. He has put you in charge of your "remnant," and He will equip you to lead them. Second, the day of "small things" is not to be disdained. He is using this time to build musical and spiritual leadership skills in you and to equip your choir to edify your church.

Many of the rehearsal techniques I'll describe work equally well with large groups. Certainly an emphasis on tone, intonation, clarity, balance, and the like are stressed in choral groups of every size. But I would like to present a few ideas that are particularly suited to small groups. I'll organize these rehearsal ideas into two main categories: (1) developing confidence and (2) building overall musicianship.

But first we'll discuss mind-set.

The Ministry Mind-set

One of the main ideas I've emphasized with my choir over the years is that we are the "lead worshipers" among our people. With so much of our rehearsal time devoted to anthems or some other type of choir feature, it's easy to fall into the trap of becoming a choral society instead of a devoted band of worship leaders.

Because it is ultimately Christ who leads us in worship each week (see Hebrews 2:12), it can be a rather daunting task to ask our congregation to stand and sing. As the leader, it's nice to know that my choir "has my back." They must come to realize that their transparent, uninhibited worship through their singing on the platform often encourages the congregation to engage their hearts as well.

Commit a portion of your rehearsal time—perhaps at the beginning of rehearsal—to singing through the corporate worship music. Decide where you will sing unison or parts. Talk about the lyrics. Discuss the design of the entire order of worship. Share with your choir the basic outline of the sermon. Pray for the service. Encourage them to lead with their hearts, souls, minds and strengths.

We are gospel communicators, not a choral club. When we transition our rehearsal into the nuts and bolt of the music, it should always be with that truth in mind. We sing in tune because we don't want to distract. We sing with good tone and balance because our message is beautiful. We express ourselves facially and with appropriate posture, because God's Word stirs emotions within us. Our performance is only for God, the "Audience of One."

Developing Confidence

Every choir has strong singers and weak ones. There will always be a wide range of innate musical ability, sight-reading skill, vocal quality, and musical knowledge. In a large group, with a few dozen people on each part, the weaker singers can "hide," singing softly and listening to the stronger folks until they gain the confidence to sing out. The small choir doesn't have that luxury.

One of the biggest fears your choir members have is to be the only one on a given part at rehearsal. You can alleviate some of the insecurity by using the techniques I'll describe next. In working with my choir for twenty years, I don't think we ever had more than twenty-five singers at rehearsal. And we've had plenty of practice sessions with fewer than a dozen. These techniques may be new to your group, but they work!

Everybody's Everything: Whenever we're working on a new piece, we all sing all the time. If it's a "ladies only" section, we all sing. "Men only," we all sing. If I want to isolate a particular part in a *divisi* section, we all sing that part. This technique allows the big choir dynamic described above to kick in throughout the rehearsal. My two or three strongest singers aren't just helping the other members of their section. They are helping everyone. Nobody gets bored or starts chatting. Everybody stays engaged.

I know what you're thinking, and I know what some of your choir members may say the first time you try this: "How am I supposed to get my part down if I'm singing everybody's part?" You'll just have to trust me. It works.

Everybody's reading ability will improve. Phrasing will begin to take on the shape of the melody, because everybody has been singing it. Range will improve, because tenors and sopranos get a chance to work on their low notes, and altos and basses get a chance to develop their upper register. Intonation improves, because a larger percentage of your rehearsal is spent in unison. Strength and endurance improve because everyone is singing throughout your rehearsal.

Have everyone sing in *his or her own octave.* When you're working on an alto line, make sure the tenors are singing in their low register, an octave below the altos. The same thing is true when you're working on a tenor line. Insist that the altos sing in their upper register, an octave above the tenors. Both of those sections would find it easier to hit the other section's notes in prime unison, but that defeats the purpose of the rehearsal technique. We want to develop range, so encourage them to sing out of their comfort zone.

There are lots of ways to go about this. In most small choir materials there is only a small section of the music that has three- or four-part *divisi*. Here's how I might work an eight-measure section of SATB with my choir.

First time—everybody sings soprano

Second time—everybody sings alto

Third time—everybody sings tenor

Fourth time—everybody sings bass

Fifth time—tenors and sopranos sing soprano; altos and basses sing alto

Sixth time—tenors and sopranos sing tenor; altos and basses sing bass

Seventh time—ladies on their normal part, all men on tenor

Eighth time—men on their normal part, all women on alto

Ninth time—everybody on his or her normal part

Each time, have your pianist accompany, not bang out the individual parts. The choir is learning to "place" their parts within a harmonic progression, not memorizing a tone row. The only time I ever have the pianist play an individual part is if the entire choir—including the director—can't get it. That almost never happens.

There are a couple of additional things that will begin to occur in your group over time that may surprise you.

First, some of your sopranos may not really be sopranos after all. They may have been singing soprano all these years because of a lack of reading ability. "I'll just sing soprano because I can hear the melody, and that's where the melody lives." As those "sopranos" get a chance to sing alto in every rehearsal, some of them will naturally gravitate to that part without a lot of arm-twisting from you.

Secondly, you'll begin to develop "rovers" in every section, men and ladies capable of singing either part. That's especially nice on the Sunday when one of your sections is "understaffed." You simply move one of your rovers to the other part.

Talking Through the Rhythms: When we are rehearsing tricky, syncopated rhythms, we tend to spend too much time talking about the *math*. The "and" of this and the "da" of that mostly confuses our nonreaders and hampers the goal of quickly getting the rhythms mastered. Most of the complex rhythms in our music are there because of the lyrics. It's what I would call "agogic" rhythms, language-based syncopation.

So I spend time on sections like this by having my choir "talk" through the rhythm while the pianist keeps time with the accompaniment. This takes the pitch distraction away and allows the group to master the rhythms before addressing the pitches.

Finding the First Pitch: One source of insecurity for your choir is making the initial entrance at the beginning of a section. Help them find that first pitch in the piano part leading into a section or from one of the other vocal parts.

Have them mark that pitch and listen for it as you're rehearsing the "everybody's everything" method above. Rather than simply playing those first pitches on the piano, have the pianist lead them into the section with the piano part.

Sequencing versus Spot Work: "Sequencing" your music is simply singing large portions without stopping, while "spot work" is stopping to isolate a problem and fix it. Sequencing solidifies a section and allows your choir to get an overall feel for the piece. Spot work—although necessary from time to time—breaks the flow of your rehearsal and stresses your singers.

Sequencing is perceived by your choir as approval; spot work as disapproval. I try to shoot for about an 80/20 relationship in my rehearsal with eighty percent sequencing. It always amazes me how many things the choir naturally fixes in a section of music on the second time through. Keep in mind that we're trying to develop confidence in our singers. The more you stop, the more they cringe.

"Form" Rehearsal: In most of our choir material there are duplicate sections. If you devote five minutes of rehearsal time to a page of SATB work, your choir may start to panic. "If that page took five minutes to master, we're going to need an hour on this tune."

After we've mastered something like this, I like to jump to the next spot where that exact same passage occurs, sing it, and then jump to the next spot. They can then see that we didn't just master one page but that we're almost done with this anthem.

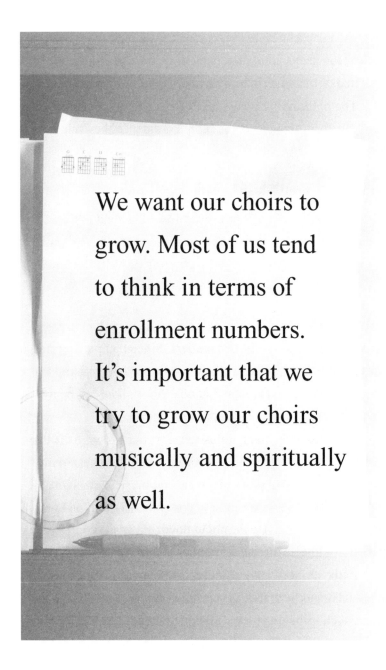

We want our choirs to grow. Most of us tend to think in terms of enrollment numbers. It's important that we try to grow our choirs musically and spiritually as well.

This is provides an opportunity to point out minor *differences* in a subsequent passage, either rhythmically or harmonically. This keeps your singers from getting too "locked in" to a particular melodic rhythm or final chord in that section.

The bottom line is that the better your singers understand the form of a piece, the more confidence they'll have in their ability to master it.

Building Overall Musicianship

We want our choirs to grow. Most of us tend to think in terms of enrollment numbers. It's important that we try to grow our choirs musically and spiritually as well. Here are a few ideas to build the musical skills of your group.

Everybody's a Reader: Most church choirs have a mixture of music readers and nonreaders. Since there are a finite number of pitches, rhythms, keys, and expressions found in our music, there's no reason that our choirs shouldn't be moving toward becoming readers all the time.

Unfortunately, many of us rehearse our groups as if they aren't capable of acquiring new skills. I tend to rehearse my groups *as if they are all readers*, calling musical elements by their real names, assuming that my nonreaders will pick up on things over time. By dumbing down our instruction, we sometimes hamstring our groups.

I talk about pitches, rhythms, expression marks, and tempo changes with the correct musical terminology, and over time the choir begins to absorb what I mean. I let them know that much of what they see on the page can be deciphered simply by watching me conduct.

Scale Degree: Rather than using some formal, complex form of referring to scale degree, I simply use numbers. When talking about chord intonation, I'll talk about who has the third. In melodic passages we identify thirds and sevenths since they have a tendency to be sung flat. I will point out steps, skips, and leaps and refer to them by number. For entrances I might say something like "Okay, gang, we're in the key of F. See the key signature at the beginning? We're entering on a C. That's the fifth in that key."

Pitch! Almost all church choirs sing flat! The higher the pitches, generally the flatter we get. Sadly, we almost never talk about it. Bands and orchestras talk about pitch all the time. The first step in fixing your choir's intonation is to discuss it.

In larger groups, bad intonation isn't as noticeable; however, it may be more crucial for the small choir. The good news is that the smaller the choir, the more time you can spend addressing this issue.

There are three ways you and your choir can begin to think about intonation issues.

First, *melodies* need to be in tune with themselves. Sing unaccompanied scales and melodies, calling attention to the scale degrees and range issues that tend to drag us down.

Second, you need to sing in tune to a *reference pitch*. I tend to talk about "placing" your sound inside the piano or inside your section. I think some of our choir members sing out of tune so they can hear themselves. Help them to understand that when your voice "disappears" into the surrounding sounds, you're singing in tune.

Third, you need to sing *chords* in tune. Point out the thirds or the "extensions" on four voice chords, and have them temper their intonation in a way that makes those chords speak.

There's an old saying in marching band circles that a straight line is the hardest thing to accomplish and the easiest to evaluate. For choirs, this is true of intonation. Nothing distracts the listener from our message more than bad pitch.

A Capella Work: Spend some portion of every rehearsal singing without accompaniment. Your choir will learn a lot about tone, intonation, vowel consistency, diction, and following a conductor by removing the "piano crutch."

Meaningful Rehearsals

For many choir members, rehearsal is the most spiritually enriching time of the week. It's important that you shepherd them with your natural personality according to your spiritual gifts. Give them time for fellowship before or after rehearsal. Allow them to share how a particular lyric has ministered to them. Tell them why you picked a particular song. Encourage them to pray for each other, for the choir to grow, for you as you lead, and that they will be a blessing to God and to your church.

Try to avoid the temptation to allow rehearsal time to be purely a musical endeavor. The greatest blessings will flow from those non-musical moments.

Youth Choir

In many small churches there aren't enough teenagers to have a youth choir. In my church, as soon as a child "ages out" of children's choir we invite him or her to join the adults.

Young voices will help your overall sound, and young people will add energy to your group. Look for spots in the music to feature just the younger voices.

The addition of youth to your adult choir can have many positive social, musical, and relational results. I place my youth between adults in our seating to facilitate the kind of mentoring we want to see take place. The adults model proper rehearsal behavior and strive to help the youth grow musically. This kind of intergenerational dynamic is described in the Pastoral Epistles of 1 and 2 Timothy and Titus.

Picking Materials

Pick some things that are easy to master, and others that will stretch your group musically. I usually keep at least ten anthems in our folders all the time. Always follow a difficult piece with lots of spot work with something they can sequence. "Sandwich" the unfamiliar with the familiar. Change styles as you progress from tune to tune. And above all, keep it moving. I try to rehearse at least six tunes per hour. They'll enjoy it more, have a more positive impression of you as a leader, and come back next week.

Blessings

I hope a few of these ideas will help as you continue to develop your small choir ministry. My prayer is that God will be honored and your church blessed by you and your choir each Sunday. Don't disdain the day of small things!

Contemplation Questions

1. Have you established a minimum number of people to be in attendance before you proceed with rehearsal?

2. Do you wait until you feel a song is "performance-ready" before you use it on Sunday, or do you stick to the schedule?

3. Are you unintentionally stressing out the non-readers?

4. Would your choir tell you they think it is your rehearsal or theirs? Is there an advantage to one over the other?

5. What do you consider "the small things"?

10

Starting and Developing a Church Instrumental Ministry

By Ed Hogan

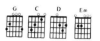

Why Do We Need Instruments?

There are plenty of pragmatic reasons for developing an instrumental ministry within your church. Instruments can add a whole new level of musical depth to the overall sound of your worship services and help facilitate a wider variety of musical styles. An instrumental ministry can also provide exciting ways for more people to use their gifts and fulfill their passions.

But I believe that a more important rationale can be found in Scripture. The New Testament doesn't have many examples of instruments being used in corporate worship. No doubt, the Early Church had little access to instrumentalists. But the Old Testament provides countless examples. Most notably, the Psalms call for a wide variety of timbres to be employed in worship. Psalm 150 lists trumpet, harp, lyre, tambourine, strings, flute, and cymbals—virtually every instrument the psalmist had available to him!

If we are to worship God "according to his excellent greatness" (Psalms 50:2), or according to His multifaceted character qualities, then we can, and should, employ every sound that can beautifully accentuate all that He is. We use a full range of dynamics, tempi, harmonics, and vocal textures. Worship should also be multi-timbral in nature.

How Do We Start?

There are many different ways to begin an instrumental ministry. Some would advocate a "shotgun" approach. Simply schedule a time for rehearsal, put an announcement in the church bulletin, and see who shows up. Many churches have used this method with varying degrees of success.

One of the problems with this approach is the wide range of experience level that may populate your ensemble from the onset. Your typical beginning band or orchestra student may not yet be ready to play in your services. More experienced players may show up without having played in years.

Another problem is the feeling of encroachment that this may cause in your current keyboardists. The sound of your piano or organ can easily become overwhelmed by the addition of even a few new players, and your present musicians will want to know exactly what role these new players will fill in the overall musical scheme.

Then there's the issue of volume. A *forte* marking on a trumpet part produces a lot more sound than the same marking in your choir. One high school player on a high G can wipe out your entire soprano section.

I'm advocating a more incremental approach to building an instrumental ministry. Start with one or two players, carefully screened and instructed. Define when they will play in the services, and find appropriate materials for them.

Let's look at this approach in more detail.

Instrumentation—Where Are We Heading?

Start by looking at what you currently have and stylistically where you are.

- Are you using piano only, piano and organ, or do you have a rhythm section?

- Is your corporate worship music mostly hymns, praise and worship songs, or a combination of the two?
- How many people are singing in your congregation?

For "piano only" congregations, adding a handful of wind instruments will be a fairly radical departure from the current sound. I would limit the initial enrollment to one or two brass or saxes, and no more than five woodwinds (flute, oboe, and clarinet). I would also use no more than two flutes and clarinets, and only one oboe.

For "piano and organ" churches, you can add a few more. The idea is not to overplay the keyboardists. The dynamic range of your instrumentalists should match what the keyboards are doing.

If you're in the process of building a rhythm section, add drums *last*. Drums with no bass will sound pretty exposed. If you have a percussionist who is ready to play, add him or her first on various traps like hand drums (djembe, bongos, congas), shaker, suspended cymbal and tambourine. Add the kit later, after you've got a solid bass and guitar sound going.

God sometimes has a tremendous sense of humor in what He may choose to provide your church. I get some pretty funny requests from folks looking for instrumental resources for odd groupings of instruments. You can make almost anything work, but before you start, think about where you're heading, or your instrumentation will get away from you pretty quickly.

Obviously, style of music will dictate what instruments you choose to use as well. A contemporary service with a romping rhythm section plus French horn may sound just as

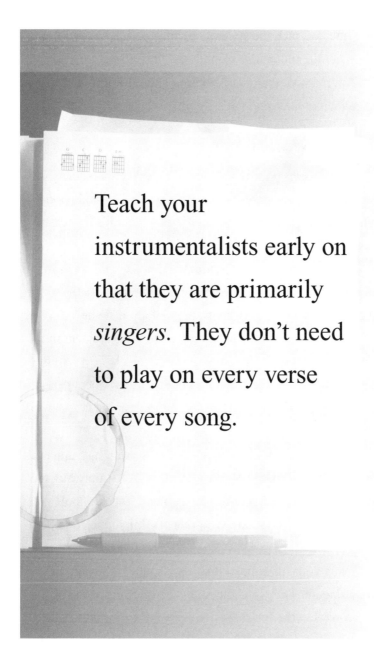

Teach your instrumentalists early on that they are primarily *singers*. They don't need to play on every verse of every song.

comical as a hymn service with pipe organ and sax quartet. Sometimes we pick the style of our music based on our personnel, not the other way around.

You'll notice that I said nothing about limiting strings. You can never have enough strings!

Where Do We Start?

Always start your instrumental ministry with *corporate worship accompaniment*. It's the easiest place to find good-quality print resources for your ensemble, and it's the least exposed type of music for the players.

There are many good hymnal and praise and worship resources fully orchestrated. Most publishers will sell you just the parts you need. Because the melody is being sung by the congregation, and the harmonic material is resident in the keyboards or rhythm section, you won't need to cover all the parts. Look for resources that do not double the vocal parts. You're looking for counter-melodic figures for the brass and woodwinds.

Budgets are usually a big issue for start-up instrumental groups, so don't buy the expensive full score. Simply buy the player's resource for his or her instrument. You can look over the instrumentalist's shoulder in rehearsal if you need to help with rhythms.

Teach your instrumentalists early on that they are primarily *singers*. They don't need to play on every verse of every song. Let the lyrics, dynamics, and style dictate who plays where, but insist that they sing when not playing. Make sure that they have the lyrics on their stand.

What Next?

After your group has become comfortable accompanying corporate singing, you might want to occasionally *feature the instrumentalists*. Preludes, offertories, and postludes are the obvious places in your order of worship, but don't forget about the sacraments. Using instruments to accompany a baptismal service or the Lord's Supper can be especially nice.

A great place to start here is with good-quality solo resources. Many different publishers have produced great arrangements for instrumentalists with piano, rhythm, or recorded tracks accompaniment.

Then, depending on your instrumentation, you might find some small-ensemble resources that will meet your needs. Add the large group features last.

Last, If Ever

Using instruments *with your vocal groups* can be tricky. As noted earlier, volume can be a real problem. There are some really nice choir anthems that have a single instrumental obbligato—such as like flute, violin or trumpet—with piano or organ. That's a good place to start. Don't let your winds cover up your choir.

How Do I Lead If I'm Not an Instrumentalist?

Vocalists are often intimidated working with instru-mentalists. They tend to fixate on mysterious transposition issues, embouchure, and instrumental pedagogy. The simplest solution is to not worry about it. Communicate with your instrumentalists the same way you would with your choir.

Talk about tone, intonation, key, dynamics, tempo, repeats, balance, and articulation, using terminology you're comfortable with.

If you hear a wrong note, talk about it in "concert pitch." If you tell a trumpeter—or some other "transposer"—that he or she played a concert F instead of concert F# in measure five, he or she should know what you mean.

Minimum Requirements for Screening Players

I recommend spending time individually with any player who wants to take part in your church instrumental ensemble. Schedule a weekly time to meet, with an accompanist present, and give the person a couple of corporate worship resources for his or her instrument. Assign a few tunes for each "lesson" based on tunes that you currently use with your church. Make sure the player knows that you intend to plug him or her into the services as soon as you're both comfortable that he or she is ready.

Spend time in each lesson having the instrumentalist play anything you've assigned plus sight-reading a few new things. You'll learn a lot in these lessons.

- Does the player have a self-starter mentality?.
- Can the player prepare pieces without a lot of help?
- How is the player's sight-reading?
- Can he or she play in tune with the piano? If not, have the player purchase an electronic tuner and get familiar with the characteristic intonation problems on his or her instrument. The player's instrument may need service as well. Help the player find a reputable instru-

ment repair shop, and get those slides pulled and pads overhauled.

- Does the player have command of all of the "church keys"? Bear in mind that most band students play in only five keys in high school: A flat, E flat, B flat, F, and C. Most high school string players will play well in A, D, G, C and F. Because church music is in eight different keys, make sure you assign some material in the keys the player isn't as familiar with. Assign scales in the unfamiliar keys as well.

- Does the player understand the transposing nature of his or her instrument? The transposing instruments are clarinet, all the saxes, trumpet, and French horn. You should be able to say, "Play a concert F," and the player should know what written pitch that is. Don't try to teach all of these. Insist that the players be able to do this for themselves. It will speed up your rehearsals if you can always talk in concert pitch.

If you can find some good solo materials with recorded accompaniment, go ahead and have the player start preparing some of those.

Once you and the player are comfortable with his or her progress, you can start using the player in your services. Don't plug him or her into your ensemble, however, until you're convinced that he or she can transpose for the instrument, handle all of the church keys, play in tune with your pianist, sight-read well enough to handle anything that comes up, and produce a pleasing tone and all the dynamic levels.

For an adult player who hasn't played since high school, it will take about six weeks before he or she can play as well as in the "glory days." Be patient and encouraging. The "chops" will come around eventually.

Have the person play only on the tunes that have been mastered, and sing on everything else. The player will develop a repertoire eventually and can then be cut loose from the lessons.

Recruiting Players

Most instrumentalists will not ask to join your group. You'll need to seek them out. Once you've found a few, your players will help you find others. Watch for people who hang around your rehearsals. You'll find clandestine players that way.

Sometimes you'll hear comments like "I used to play in high school, but I'm sure I could never do that again." That's an instrumentalist's way of asking to join your group.

They'll appreciate knowing that you're setting up lessons. That will help them know that you're not going to throw them out in front of the church until they're ready. Any player who is "too accomplished a musician" to spend some time playing for you probably isn't.

A Servant's Heart

Instrumentalists are wonderful people to work with. You'll find them to be some of your most dedicated musicians. Most will have a humble, teachable spirit. If you demonstrate a servant's heart, you'll enjoy the players God sends you.

Get Help

There are lots of good print resources for your players. There are much more comprehensive materials for helping you grow in your knowledge of instrumental music. Your local band or orchestra director can be a big help. You can also call some other churches in your area that have existing programs. You're not in this alone.

Enjoy What God Is Doing

If God is leading you to develop an instrumental ministry, know up front that it will be a fun adventure, and your church will be edified by the presence of strong players in your midst. "Let everything that has breath praise the LORD" (Psalm 150:6).

Contemplation Questions

1. Do you see an instrumental ministry as a real ministry or just one more thing to add to your plate?

2. If you know of a great player but also know he or she comes with an attitude, is that a tradeoff you are willing to make?

3. If you cannot add the instruments in the right order, would you rather wait until you have all the pieces or go ahead and use what you have?

4. If you can find someone who will serve as band leader, are you willing to turn loose of any responsibilities?

5. Have you thought about where you would go for help when you need it?

11
The Gift
of Pain

You just don't feel like leading worship today. It doesn't mean you love the Lord any less than before, but you certainly don't feel the song as you should. If you could, you would change all the songs to ballads because that's what you're feeling right now.

As I completed the final chapters of this book, I received the phone call no one wants to get and for which no one is prepared. It was from a pastor friend in Oklahoma. I couldn't make out all he was saying, but this much I did get: "Jennie has cancer." To be honest, I didn't really need to hear anything else. At that moment, the only appropriate words seemed to be none at all, so I listened.

I'm not sure there are ever the right words to say to a dad who is losing his daughter. Here was a man who already knew any scripture I could have quoted and already believed every promise I could have offered up. It is one thing to preach about the peace that passes understanding, but another thing entirely to live it out. Unsure who to lift up first, I just prayed and let God prioritize the list. I prayed for God to heal Jennie and to give wisdom to the doctors and comfort to a congregation—but a big part of my heart grieved for and with a wounded pastor.

What happens when the messenger is broken? If you have been in any level of ministry for any level of time, you have undoubtedly wrestled with this dilemma. Although I am not wise enough to understand pain, I am rich enough to have experienced it. And while some may question the place of this topic in a book for ministers of music, to me it can greatly affect how we approach worship. At some point in our ministry, each of us must ask ourselves how much of what we are dealing with is appropriate to bring to the platform. One of the threads woven throughout this book has been the importance of authenticity, and it seems especially significant when it comes to how we approach the subject of pain.

The obvious right answer is that there is no obvious right answer. I have known some worship leaders who could lead a perfectly normal service with the congregation never suspecting there is a struggle taking place in the worship leader's life. I have also witnessed others who felt it their solemn duty to lower the entire congregation into their own depths of personal darkness—all in the spirit of authenticity. With one extreme, we risk cheating true believers out of real faith opportunities, while the other extreme can potentially deprive a worshiper of the joy of worship.

I ask you to allow me some personal latitude in this discussion—not because I think my approach is the only right one, but rather because this is an area in which I am particularly passionate. In return, I will do my best to establish relevance between personal pain and true worship.

A close friend recently sent me a text that said, "I do not want any more emotion. I just want happy." My response was that the last time I checked, happy was an emotion too. After the ensuing banter I began to think about how much richer I am for every emotion I have ever experienced. Because of fear, I have learned more about my insecurities; through anger I have become better at forgiveness. I doubt it would surprise anyone who knows me to discover that the emotion that has had the most profound effect on me is sorrow. Not only has it defined in large measure who I am personally, but in the process it has deepened my understanding of the power of grace.

While physical suffering has largely driven my own encounters with sorrow, that certainly is not the only potential source. And although I am not a counselor, I have noticed a consistent trend through my own journey. My deepest exposures to sorrow have almost always served as the means to new beginnings.

Let me say it another way. I have never known God to waste any pain in my life. What He has trusted me with He has prepared me for, walked beside me through, and found a way to use for His glory. I am not saying I am where James tells me I should be when he wrote that we should endure suffering and count it all joy. I honestly wish I could say that, but I'm not there yet. I do, however, find it interesting that in James 5:13 when he tells those who are suffering to pray, he immediately follows it up by encouraging the cheerful to sing songs of praise. In my life the two have always been inexplicably connected. It seems the richest songs have always been born out of the greatest sorrow. It has allowed me to learn, taught me to trust, and, yes, prepared me to lead worship.

I began this chapter with a discussion of what is appropriate to bring to the platform. For me, the answer is all of it. I cannot separate how I lead from where God has led me. It is imbedded into the very marrow of who I am. And for those of you who have walked through your own valley of the shadow, you have already discovered the transformation that takes place in both the message and the messenger. Firsthand grief allows the message to come alive in ways you could not have

Because of His sacrifice
for us, we can go to
the altar of God with
exceeding joy, and we
praise Him for who
He is and what He has
delivered us from.

imagined and prepares the messenger to minister to those who grieve with a greater depth of compassion than possible before.

As I stated earlier, this book is not intended to be an attempt at theology, and that goes for dealing with pain as well. But I would encourage you to take a few minutes to examine what effect sorrow has had on how you lead worship. How has it affected your level of faith? Has the pain you experienced come primarily from within, or has suffering resulted from the tough places of those directly under your ministry?

I had been at a church only four months when one of our band members was arrested and sent to jail. Nothing anyone had told me could have prepared me for something of this nature. I watched and learned as my pastor counseled without condemnation, and during that process both the message and the messenger were transformed. On another occasion, one of our choir families lost a father and was blessed with a baby in the span of one week. Once again, somewhere in between the joy and the sorrow, the worship of the lead worshiper took on a new dimension. I have seen families divided by divorce in which the pain I experienced seemed as intense as anything I had ever been through physically. Yet through it all I was reminded that we worship a Man of Sorrows who is acquainted with our grief.

One more time let's revisit the initial question of this chapter: *How does the gift of pain affect your offering of praise?* I already said that we should bring to the act of worship everything God has created us to be. Now let me take it one step further by saying I do not believe worship is—nor was ever intended to be—about us. It is all about Him. When I suggest that worship requires all of who I am, the emphasis is on the word *all* rather than the words *who I am*. The song is His, and only by His grace and through His mercy does He allow me to lift it.

And so we come each and every Sunday—from those assembled in the small storefront sanctuaries to imposing brick buildings with towering steeples. Because of His sacrifice for us, we can go to the altar of God with exceeding joy, and we praise Him for who He is and what He has delivered us from. We enter His gates with thanksgiving and His courts with praise!

> Praise the Lord.
>> Praise God in his sanctuary;
>> praise him in his mighty heavens.
>
> Praise him for his acts of power;
>> praise him for his surpassing greatness.
>
> Praise him with the sounding of the trumpet,
>> praise him with harp and lyre,
>
> praise him with tambourine and dancing,
>> praise him with the strings and flute,
>
> praise him with the clash of cymbals,
>> praise him with resounding cymbals.
>
> Let everything that has breath praise the Lord.
>> Praise the Lord *(Psalm 150)*.

The Promise: "God is our refuge and strength, an ever-present help in trouble. Therefore we will not fear, though the earth give way and the mountains fall into the heart of the sea, though its waters roar and foam and the mountains quake with their surging" (Psalm 46:1-3).

The Prayer: *Lord, today I stand unworthy yet come boldly into your presence. Take me as I am, and use me for service. May the Giver of the song be evident in my midnight hour. All the glory and the honor and the praise is yours alone.*

Contemplation Questions

1. When you're dealing with pain, is your first reaction to hide it?

2. Do you feel there is a right or wrong time to let the church in on your hurt?

3. Do you have the strength to be an encourager even when you are hurting?

4. When you are hurting, do you try to choose songs that help you heal or help you forget?

5. What is the effect of pain on what we bring to worship?

12

The Golden Hour

It's Easter Sunday evening, and you are completely worn out. In the last few months you have rehearsed and directed two musicals, coordinated costumes, including everything from shepherds to Roman soldiers, and now you need a Sunday off. Someone asked you today if you are doing a Fourth of July musical. Wrong question, wrong day!

I am not quite sure when, but somewhere through the years of traveling in music ministry it dawned on me that I had fallen into a familiar routine when visiting a church for the first time. I would start out walking around the platform as though I believed that if I stood there long enough I might gain some insight into what kind of people would be there. I looked at music on the piano, wandered through the choir room, and usually ended up at the sound booth. The truth is, I probably did this not so much for what I would learn but because I was curious by nature.

Years ago I had the opportunity to minister at a small Nazarene church in South Carolina. One Sunday I got there early and as usual started through my paces when something unique caught my eye. Attached to the small wooden pulpit was a laminated piece of paper the size of a bumper sticker with a picture of a clock and the words *The Golden Hour.* In a slightly smaller type below, it said, "We have one hour to make a difference in someone's life."

I stopped and just looked at it for a few minutes before I moved on. As I walked toward the piano, I saw the same cardboard reminder there as well. By now the wheels were beginning to turn a little faster. As I continued walking, I found the same thing at the organ, the music stand facing the choir,

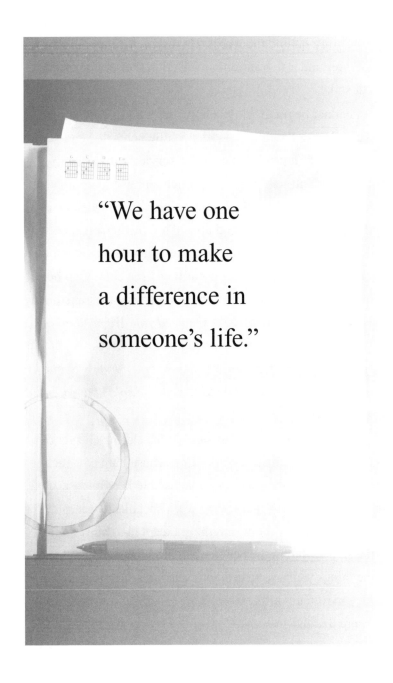

"We have one
hour to make
a difference in
someone's life."

and even the audio console. When the pastor arrived, I asked him the story behind the words. He responded that it was just a subtle reminder to everyone involved in the service of what was at stake.

I cannot begin to tell you how many times down through the years I have thought about those little notes. When I see a musician walk in just in time for the service with what appears to be an attitude in tow, or watch a praise team singer who seems preoccupied with something besides worship, everything in me wants to stand up and tell the person about the golden hour. When the audio operator is not paying attention to what is happening on the platform or I see choir members with their heads buried in their books, I have a message on my heart for them. The message is *We need you. We need all of you. We need everyone involved to take on a Kingdom philosophy that compels you to stay focused on not only the task but also the opportunity at hand. One hour holds the potential for an eternal impact.*

Why would I include this story in the closing chapter of a book directed to ministers of music? Because I am convinced sometimes *we* are the very ones who need to hear it most. If we are not careful, the one day of the week specifically set aside for worship can easily become anything except that. Most of the loving saints who fill the pews do not have the slightest clue of all the things you have to deal with and stress about on a typical Sunday morning. Furthermore, it is part of your responsibility to ensure that they don't.

When I first started leading worship, one of the biggest surprises to me was the discovery of how many people it took for Sunday morning to happen. The second surprise was how much twenty or so minutes of music a week required from me. It can be all-consuming and, as you also know, even part-time ministry has an effect on the entire family. It is assumed your spouse is part of the package when you come to work, even when the package is a volunteer one. Because you have to be there so early on Sunday morning, you and your family usually come and leave in separate cars, and you do not have any time to spend with them either before or after the service due to all the details demanding your attention. Does this sound familiar?

A tough reality check for me was when our son Sam was about four years old. A mother of one of the other kids in his Sunday School class told me something she thought was funny, yet it gnawed at me for a long time. She said her daughter was talking about Sam one Sunday afternoon at their dinner table and said, "Sam doesn't have a daddy." The mother said she tried to correct her daughter but finally asked her why she thought that. Her response was "Because only his mommy ever comes to get him from class." While I could make a pretty compelling argument as to why that is just the way things are, I could not get the little girl's comments out of my mind. The sad reality I had to come to grips with was that I did not even know where Sam's Sunday School classroom was.

Have you ever had this conversation with your spouse? Have you ever stopped to think if possibly you are just as guilty as the church when it comes to making assumptions about your family's commitment?

I am assuming that almost any worship leader reading this book can relate to the previous two paragraphs. I am also assuming those same readers know that I am not complaining. As we have discovered, the blessings of the call far outweigh the occasional seasons of discouragement. One of the greatest experiences for any worship leader is the moment we did not or could not plan for happens, and we get to experience it from the best seat in the house. Not only do we get to witness the impact of the golden hour, but somehow in the process, every now and then we also become the recipient, and it is we who are changed in the process. Just what we need, just when we need it!

When I first began working on this book, I wrote down on a piece of paper three words—three goals—that I hoped to accomplish in these pages.

The first of these words is *educate.* I heard a statistic at a conference a few weeks ago that seventy-five percent of the churches in the United States average less than two hundred in attendance. When I heard that, I went back and looked at the topics in this book one more time. What was I missing? What do I wish someone had taught me when I first started that was not in a textbook?

If the seventy-five percent statistic is true—and I have no reason to doubt it is—then I fear something may be missing when it comes to how we are supposed to learn. Let's face it. There is no shortage of training available for ministers of music. Some of you had the benefit of learning from a college class or doing an internship. There are seminars available and web sites filled with advice, but the bulk of what I found was geared toward large church programs and philosophies. I could not go to the neighborhood bookstore and find anything to explain the benefits of filling out a CCLI report, nor could I find a Twelve-Step program that taught conflict resolution techniques in a church where half of the people are related. Who do you ask what to do when you feel that the senior pastor says he or she has your back but sometimes you wonder?

For many years I have been blessed to have opportunities to speak at songwriting seminars around the country. I realize going into each class that it's impossible to turn a roomful of people into great songwriters in an hour and a half. Therefore, even though I spend a lot of time going over the basic techniques of songwriting, the real goal is to inspire them about the process. If I can accomplish that, they have the potential to go out and become great songwriters. The point I am trying to make is that I can provide the tools, but they have to build the house themselves. What they discover is that the real education comes in the application.

When our son Sam was still pretty young, we were driving down the road one day, and he was looking out the window, as little kids tend to do. We passed a house with a bundle of lumber stacked at the end of the driveway, and Sam said, "Look, Dad—they're growing a swing set." Although I laughed then, I have thought about his words periodically through the years. Have I been guilty of the same way of thinking? Have I ordered the lumber as if the swing set would build itself? Have I bought books or taken classes that were intended to make me better at what God called me to do, yet I continued doing what I do just as I have always done it?

My friend Stan Endicott—a driving force behind the early days of Maranatha! Music—is one of the funniest, most creative people I have ever known. I have watched him hold a roomful people spellbound with his insights, even when at times I was convinced he was making the stuff up as he went along. When he talks, he speaks in what I call "Stanisms"—little nuggets that hold great insight. I try to remember as many of them as possible when he says them, because, to tell the truth, I am not convinced he will remember what he said when he is done. Because Stan is a mentor by his very nature and has a heart for the small church, I felt it important to include some random Stanisms for your perusal:

- The best way to have a great idea is to have a lot of ideas.
- People don't get better all at once.
- You can't learn from people just like you.
- We can't make things grow; we can only prepare the soil.
- Get ready for change. You have about a week.

If we are truly serious about worshiping where we are planted, each of these lines merits a good amount of consideration. Whether taken one line at a time or collectively, they offer great insight into the task we are all faced with as worship pastors. In this changing world of worship music, if we do not continue to learn, we are all but guaranteed to find ourselves looking for something to do on Sunday. Change not only is coming—it has happened in the time it has taken you to read this book.

I think it is great and wonderful that you know the difference between conducting a 6/8 and a 3/4 song. If you know how to write a glissando in an orchestra score, I think that is awesome. However, if your group is trying to figure out what it means to clap on the beat versus off the beat, it might be time to put this book down and simply lead them from your heart.

Every person you come in contact with enters the sanctuary from a different avenue of life. I do not need to remind you that change means something different to each of them. Be willing to love them, lead them, and learn from them in the process. Some of the wisest leaders I have known through the years have also been the most vulnerable.

How long has it been since those you lead have seen you vulnerable? Do you sometimes feel that to be a leader you always have to have it all together on the platform? If we aren't careful, we can drift into what I call Kodak worship moments. You know the ones I am referring to—where the very instant the service begins we transform ourselves into the quintessential worship leader. We have learned to stand the right way, lift our hands at the proper moments, say everything a worship leader is supposed to say, and still be guilty of imitation rather than authentic worship.

How long has it been since you thought about your definition of worship? When someone asks how you define it, what is your response? Unfortunately, the typical answer to the question has too often been reduced to a style of music or, in some cases, even tempo of music. Given enough time, we could probably all come up with a biblically appropriate answer, so let me ask it in a different way: How do you *live* worship? Is it truly a lifestyle, or is it twenty minutes of music on Sunday morning?

I have read numerous books and articles through the years in my attempt to define what worship really is. If I didn't know better, I might wonder if the goal of each new explanation is to try to confuse the listener even more. I'll let theologians who are more skilled than I solve that puzzle, but I do have some thoughts for the purpose of this book:

I don't want to merely *attend* worship—I want to *experience* it.

I can most effectively lead worship by setting the example as the lead worshiper.

Worship music is not intended to entertain the worshipers but rather to please a holy God.

Worship should never be about my comfort level or my musical tastes. It should be a gift from the creation to the Creator.

It is only through His righteousness that we are able to come into His presence, and we do so humbly and with reverence.

Several years ago my long-time friend and mentor Jim Van Hook and I attended an event in Nashville billed as a worship experience.

Jim is one of those people who has a gift for skillfully articulating any situation, and that night was no exception. I doubt I will ever forget his summation of the evening. He said, "Worship should never be the event. Worship must always be the response."

In John 4:23, Jesus says, "Yet a time is coming and has now come when the true worshipers will worship the Father in spirit and truth; for they are the kind of worshipers the Father seeks." The key is that God desires us to respond in both spirit and truth, which is the true way He desires to be worshiped.

I challenge each of you who read these pages to ask yourself this question: *Am I planning an event, or am I willing to be a leader in the response?* The response of authentic worship can and should be both personal and public, individual and corporate, but most of all genuine.

Even though most of this book has been devoted to improving ministry technique, we must be careful to guard against the human elements of ministry distracting from the authenticity of our worship.

The second word on my list is *engage.* I have filled these pages with my own theories, ideas, and philosophies. Neither the goal nor the assumption, however, was that this would become the final word in any discussion of how to be a better worship leader. The hope was that in reacting to what I wrote, you would engage in the dialog. As you react to my ideas, be deliberate in developing your own. Talk about it with those close to you whom you know you can trust—people who share your heart for the mission.

That may be your senior pastor. I had a friend tell me before I took my first assignment never to take a church based on the people but rather the relationship with the senior pastor. It was good advice that seemed even more insightful through the years that followed. If that is your situation, set aside some time on a regular basis when the only agenda is to dialog.

For others, the dialog may begin at home. My wife is a junior highschool math teacher in a public school. Although she has never written a song or, to my knowledge, directed a choir, she is still at the top of my list when it comes to sounding boards. The point is that you need someone to hold you accountable when it comes to raising the standard.

If it can't be someone who knows you well, the next best thing is to find someone who is familiar with the expectations, the pressures, and the payoffs of a church position, perhaps another minister of music in town. I have seen situations where a lunch with a fellow minister of music led to a monthly lunch that included several worship pastors. If you can pull that off, leave your pride and whatever competitive thoughts and nature behind. It is one kingdom, and we are all on the same team.

The third word on my initial list of goals is the one I will leave you with: *encourage*. It doesn't matter if you are leading worship in a start-up church that meets in your den or the big church on the corner—each and every one of us wonders from time to time if anybody hears what we are saying or gets what we are doing. Sometimes the encouragement we need most comes simply from knowing we are not alone in the battle.

I initially assumed that one of the downsides to leading at a smaller church would be all the other things I would have to do besides the actual music part. Sure enough, there were days I found myself in a hospital waiting room making conversation with people I barely knew, or trading what would have been a perfectly good day of golf with sitting in a meeting discussing how to pay for the broken heat and air conditioning unit at the church. When I look back, however, I can see God's hand in all of it. Rather than seeing it as a downside, I realize some of the moments I was encouraged most was when God put me in the place of being the encourager.

Most of you know what I am talking about—those moments in the course of ministry when God uses the very ones you thought you were supposed to minister to as a means of ministering to you. There is an old line I have used with young songwriters for years: "When the student is ready, the teacher appears." Even though I do not understand how it works, I just know it does. When a writer has honed the craft to the point that it is ready, somehow, some way, it always finds its way to the right person.

In the same way, I have spent most of my life either serving in ministry or working alongside those who do. If there is one thing I have learned for certain, it is that when the servant is weary, God sends an encourager. The encouragement does not always come in ways we expect or with words we want to hear, but God is always faithful to meet the needs of those who are called according to His purpose.

I want to close with one final story. Several years ago I was ministering at a small church just north of Nashville, where I live. At the end of the service I sat at the piano doing a closing song, and the Holy Spirit took over. People began to come forward to pray, and the presence of God permeated the small sanctuary. Because I was never blessed with a huge amount of natural talent as a singer and was an average musician at best, I think I enjoyed those moments so much because I knew it was not about anything I had done. As I sat there a few feet from the front row, yet in the center of God's presence, I was overwhelmed by what I was witnessing. I don't know that I have ever felt both so humbled at God's majesty and so blessed by His call on my life.

The result of that evening was a song I ended up finishing with two good friends, Tony Wood and Don Koch. I leave you with the lyrics to that song and a prayer of blessing on you, your family, your ministry, and your call. I pray it will bring you encouragement in the days ahead when you need it most, I pray you never lose the sense of awe at being called, and most of all, I pray that you never stop hearing the music God placed in your heart.

I Was in the Room

The church is empty but I just can't go home
So I linger for a moment in the dark all alone
And I'm so overwhelmed at how your spirit moved
I'm just glad
I was in the room

So many stories and no one knows but you
The silent prayers answered tonight in these pews
And I don't understand how you do what you do
I'm just glad
I was in the room

Great God in heaven
How wonderful you are
Oh you're still changing lives
And it humbles my heart

That you would allow someone like me
To play a small part

So tonight as I stand here I'm reminded once more
That when any good happens it's not about me Lord
It's enough that I stand in the shadow of you
I'm just glad
I was in the room

The Promise: "The LORD your God is with you, he is mighty to save. He will take great delight in you, he will quiet you with his love, he will rejoice over you with singing (Zephaniah 3:17).

The Prayer: *Lord, I pray that you will bless us with your presence, strengthen us with your promise, and rejoice over our efforts with your singing.*

Contemplation Questions

1. How long has it been since you felt God break through to you as you led?

2. Is your spouse as committed to your call as you are? What about your children?

3. Is the call still as vibrant as it was when you began?

4. If you were to come up with some of your own "Stanisms," what would they be?

5. Is your worship an event or a response?

About the Contributor

ED HOGAN received a degree from Florida State University, where he studied music education and composition. He was a high school band director for eleven years before founding EHF Productions, Inc., a full-service music and audio production company. Besides serving as Instrumental Editor and Consultant for Lillenas, Ed arranges, orchestrates, and does Finale engraving for several church music publishers. He frequently serves as a clinician at reading sessions, workshops, and conferences. He and his wife, Carol, live in Carrollton with their daughters, Katie and Caroline.

THE LATEST PRAISE & WORSHIP SONGS . . . ALL IN ONE BOOK!

→ 118 favorites for congregation, worship team, or small group use in easy-to-read songbook format

→ 63 song titles are provided in split-channel format for pre-recorded accompaniment options

→ Now with complete church-friendly orchestrations

All the Best Songs of Praise & Worship 3

Here is another great release from the immensely popular *All the Best Songs of Praise & Worship* series. You will find this ultimate gathering of songs chosen from the trusted Top 500 CCLI to be invaluable for congregational worship as well as for solo presentation.